Baker's
Worship Handbook

Also by Paul E. Engle

Baker's
Worship Handbook

Traditional and Contemporary Service Resources

Paul E. Engle

Baker Books

A Division of Baker Book House Co
Grand Rapids, Michigan 49516

© 1998 by Paul E. Engle

Published by Baker Books
a division of Baker Book House Company
P.O. Box 6287, Grand Rapids, MI 49516-6287

Fourth printing, November 2003

Printed in the United States of America

Library of Congress Cataloging-in-Publication Data

Baker's worship handbook : traditional and contemporary service resources / [edited by] Paul E. Engle.
    p.   cm.
    Includes bibliographical references.
    ISBN 0-8010-9050-4 (cloth)
    1. Public worship—Handbooks, manuals, etc. I. Engle, Paul E.
BV25.B35   1998
264—dc21   97-46610

For current information about all releases from Baker Book House, visit our web site:
               http://www.bakerbooks.com

To
Christine
and
Heather

Contents

Contents

Preface

A familiar scene is repeated each Friday in countless church offices. The secretary needs to complete the church bulletin but has not yet received the necessary information on the order of worship from the pastor or music director. Prompted by the secretary's gentle reminder, the pastor takes ten hurried minutes from a busy schedule to pencil some hymn numbers and Scripture references on a copy of last week's bulletin. The pressured leader then resumes sermonic research, makes a hospital call, keys in some letters on the computer, reads and replies to waiting e-mail, and finally conducts a premarital counseling interview that evening. The next time the pastor looks over the order of worship is Sunday morning.

Are the planning and preparation for worship so marginally important as to warrant only that minimal amount of attention? Or should corporate worship remain the highest priority for each local Christian community in the new millennium?

Consider these reasons for the centrality of corporate worship: Sunday worship is generally the only occasion at which the entire church family is together at the same time and place. For many visitors it's the entry point into the church—the means by which they evaluate whether or not they'll return. It is not surprising that corporate worship has also been historically linked to great times of spiritual revival in the history of the church. When revival broke out in Jonathan Edwards' church in Northampton, Massachusetts, during the Great Awakening of the 1700s, he noted the impact on his church's Sunday services: "The town seemed to be full of the presence of God. . . . Our public assemblies were then beautiful: the congregation was alive in God's service, every one earnestly intent on the public worship, every hearer eager to drink in the words of the minister as they came from his mouth; the assembly in general were, from time to time, in tears while the word was preached; . . . Our public praises were then greatly enlivened."[1]

Sunday worship is also worthy of our diligent attention because it is a potential land mine for conflict in the church, a place where the archenemy can often gain a toehold. Sunday worship both shapes and reflects the view of God held by the members of the congregation. It colors all the other functions and activities of the church. Planning and leading worship with competence is a means of fulfilling the teaching of Scripture that we assemble for worship on the first day of each week. "True worshipers will worship the Father in spirit and truth, for they are the kind of worshipers the Father seeks" (John 4:23). Think of it—the Father actively seeks our worship!

If that weren't enough to motivate careful planning for worship services, we need to remember that Sunday worship services are a prime way to prepare for what will engage us for eternity. "Worship is the supreme and only indispensable activity of the Christian Church. It alone will endure . . . into heaven when all other activities of the Church will have passed away."[2] Therefore we dare not be slipshod or complacent about the high and holy privilege of planning and leading the church in corporate worship.

✝ Why This Book Was Written

Baker's Worship Handbook was written to provide Christian leaders with a comprehensive reference tool to prepare and plan a variety of God-centered worship services including the Lord's Supper, baptisms, infant dedications, confirmations and public professions of faith, anointings of the sick, recognition of births and adoptions, groundbreakings, and church building dedications. Resources for regular Sunday worship services include prayer helps, doxologies, affirmations of faith, offering resources, music resources, and thirty thematic guides to the acts and attributes of God. These thematic guides include call to worship texts, responsive calls to worship, and prayers of adoration. Within the space of a single volume Christian leaders can find numerous resources to use in developing creative services, whatever one's denomination or tradition. This volume forms a natural companion to *Baker's Wedding Handbook* and *Baker's Funeral Handbook*.

✝ Who Can Use This Book

This handbook was written with the following people in mind:

- Pastors of many different denominations who can find resources from which to plan weekend worship services, whether traditional, contemporary, or blended
- Music directors and worship leaders who have responsibility for planning weekly services
- Worship committee members and planning committees/teams who are looking for fresh resources to add variety to services
- Church staff members who are responsible for planning and leading special services such as baptisms, confirmations, dedications, hymn festivals, and the other occasions for which this volume provides examples
- Ministerial students who are learning how to plan for worship occasions in the church

✝ Trans-Denominational, Contemporary, and Traditional Styles

Recent years have witnessed a blurring of denominational distinctives in worship styles. Cultural shifts have contributed to the emergence of new models of worship including seeker-driven, seeker-sensitive, blended, and contemporary experimental models alongside traditional, historical, charismatic, and liturgical models. Shifting styles of music have strongly influenced worship in many churches. Whether one's church prefers services characterized as contemporary or traditional, informal or formal, high-culture or pop-culture, helpful resources in this volume can be used to plan next weekend's services. Appendixes include valuable charts, forms, and resources which may be photocopied.

 A Personal Word

Baker's Worship Handbook comes out of the author's front-line experience in planning and leading worship services, working with music directors and worship planning groups, teaching worship courses in several seminaries, conducting local church worship seminars, and observing the changing worship scene in a cross section of churches while serving as a guest preacher.

I am grateful for those who have influenced me through the years, thereby contributing directly and indirectly to this volume. These include my father, who served as my first pastor; members and officers in the churches I have pastored; faculty members during my doctoral studies on worship at Westminster Theological Seminary; seminary students with whom I have interacted in the classes I have taught over the years; individuals who raised stimulating questions in the worship seminars I have conducted; and pastor friends who provided ideas—some of which found their way into this volume. I am especially thankful to my wife, Margie, for her invaluable contributions to the writing of this book.

Planning and leading God-centered services of worship are among the highest privileges that belong to church leaders. This handbook is offered to the glory of God with the prayer that you will find in its pages valuable resources and ideas which will enable you to encourage God's people to offer worship in spirit and truth—preparing us for what we will be privileged to enjoy for eternity.

"Now glory be to God! By his mighty power at work within us, he is able to accomplish infinitely more than we would ever dare to ask or hope. May he be given glory in the church and in Christ Jesus forever and ever through endless ages. Amen" (Ephesians 3:20–21 NLT).

[1] Jonathan Edwards, *A Narrative of Surprising Conversions* (Edinburgh: Banner of Truth Trust, 1736), p. 14.

[2] William Nicholls, *Jacob's Ladder: The Meaning of Worship* (Richmond: John Knox Press, 1958), p. 9.

PART 1

Worship Planning Resources

1

Prayers for Corporate Worship

✝ Invocations and Opening Prayers

Almighty God, unto whom all hearts are open, all desires known, and from whom no secrets are hid; Cleanse the thoughts of our hearts by the inspiration of thy Holy Spirit, that we may perfectly love thee, and worthily magnify thy holy Name; through Christ our Lord. Amen (*Book of Common Prayer*, 1952).

Our Father, to whom belongs our adoration and praise, we ask that you will prepare us, through the presence of your Spirit, to come before you worthily and to ask of you rightly. May all who worship with us this day present their bodies as a living sacrifice, holy, acceptable to you. Shed your light on our human understanding, cleanse our desires and motives, stir our wills to obedience to your Word. Direct that your name might be exalted this hour in this assembly.

May our worship glorify you, through Jesus Christ our Lord. Amen.

Almighty God, Who hast given us grace at this time with one accord to make our common supplications unto Thee and does promise that when two or three are gathered together in Thy name Thou wilt grant their requests; fulfill now, O Lord, the desires and petitions of Thy servants, as may be most expedient for them; granting us in this world knowledge of Thy truth, and in the world to come life everlasting. Amen (Chrysostom).

Great art thou, O Lord, and greatly to be praised; great is thy power, and thy wisdom is infinite. Thee would we praise without ceasing. Thou callest us to delight in thy praise, for thou hast made us for thyself, and our hearts find no rest until we rest in thee; to whom with the Father and the Holy Spirit all glory, praise, and honor be ascribed, both now and forevermore. Amen (St. Augustine).

✝ Prayers of Confession

Almighty and most merciful Father; We have erred, and strayed from thy ways like lost sheep. We have followed too much the devices and desires of our own hearts. We have offended against thy holy laws. We have left undone those things which we ought to have done; And we have done those things which we ought not to have done; And there is no health in us. But thou, O Lord, have mercy upon us, miserable offenders. Spare thou those, O God, who confess their faults. Restore thou those who are penitent; According to thy promises declared unto mankind in Christ Jesus our Lord. And grant, O most merciful Father, for his sake; That we may hereafter live a godly, righteous, and sober life. To the glory of thy holy Name. Amen (*BCP*, 1952).

O Lord, have mercy on us, according to your steadfast love; according to your great mercies, blot out our transgressions. Wash us thoroughly from our iniquity, and cleanse us from our sin. For we are aware of our transgressions, and our sin is ever before our thoughts. Create in us a clean heart, O God, and put a new and right spirit within us. Cast us not away from your presence, and take not your Holy Spirit from us. Restore to us the joy of your salvation, and uphold us with a willing spirit. This we pray in the name of Jesus Christ our Lord (Adapted from Psalm 51).

O Lord God, eternal and almighty Father, we confess and acknowledge unfeignedly before thy holy majesty that we are poor sinners, conceived and born in iniquity and corruption, prone to do evil, incapable of any good, and that in our depravity we transgress thy holy commandments without end or ceasing: Wherefore we purchase for ourselves, through thy righteous judgment, our ruin and perdition. Nevertheless, O Lord, we are grieved that we have offended thee; and we condemn ourselves and our sins with true repentance, beseeching thy grace to relieve our distress.

O God and Father most gracious and full of compassion, have mercy upon us in the name of thy Son, our Lord Jesus Christ. And as thou dost blot out our sins and stains, magnify and increase in us day by day the grace of thy Holy Spirit: that as we acknowledge our unrighteousness with all our heart, we may be moved by that sorrow which shall bring forth true repentance in us, mortifying all our sins, and producing in us the fruits of righteousness and innocence which are pleasing unto thee; through the same Jesus Christ our Lord. Amen (John Calvin, quoted in Bard Thompson, *Liturgies of the Western Church*, pp. 197–98).

Lord God, we confess our failure to be true even to our own accepted standards, our unwillingness to apply to ourselves the standards of conduct we demand of others, our complacency towards wrongs that do not touch our own lives, our slowness to see the good in others and the evil in ourselves, our hardness of heart toward the faults of our neighbors and our readiness to make allowances for our own. O Lord, please forgive and grant us your pardon through Christ. Amen.

Almighty Father, we enter your presence confessing the things we try to conceal from you and the things we try to conceal from others. We confess the heartbreak, worry, and sorrow we have caused, that make it difficult for others to forgive us, the times we have made it easy for others to do wrong, the harm we have done that makes it hard for us to forgive ourselves. Lord have mercy and forgive us through Christ. Amen.

Lord God, we confess that we are prone to ease and pleasure, adverse to self-discipline and sacrifice, anxious to hear new things, yet indifferent to the good news of Christ. We confess that we are enthusiastic in getting, cautious in giving, eager in amusement, lazy in service, quick to anger, slow to forgive, ready to promise, but reluctant to perform. We admit our sins and ask that in your mercy you might pardon us through Christ. Amen.

Confession Using Beatitudes (NLT)

Leader: God blesses those who realize their need for him, for the Kingdom of Heaven is given to them.

People: But we have been proud in spirit, inflated with pride in our own self-sufficiency. We have forgotten how needy we are.

Leader: God blesses those who mourn, for they will be comforted.

People: But we have not mourned over our sins, instead we have insulated ourselves from those around us, from their pain, needs, loneliness, and suffering. We have even hardened ourselves so that we are unaware that our own lives cause grief to the Lord.

Leader: God blesses those who are gentle and lowly, for the whole earth will belong to them.

People: But we have valued toughness over gentleness. We have too often chosen to be concerned with ourselves rather than our brothers and sisters and neighbors. Like the prodigal son, we want to satisfy ourselves rather than our Father.

Leader: God blesses those who are hungry and thirsty for justice, for they will receive it in full.

People: But instead we have hungered after the pleasures, prestige, and possessions of this temporal world. Like Esau we too have despised our birthright by choosing to satisfy our immediate desires.

Leader: God blesses those who are merciful, for they will be shown mercy.

People: But we have too often presided as harsh judges over the lives of others. We have been quick to place blame on anything or anyone but ourselves. We have avoided any obligation to care or to help those in need.

Leader: God blesses those whose hearts are pure, for they will see God.

People: But we have defiled our hearts with idols of our own choosing, doubting that God will keep his Word and his promises. We continually compromise the truth by trying to find meaning and security in our jobs, our friends, our pleasures, and our projects—but not in God.

Leader: God blesses those who work for peace, for they will be called the children of God.

People: But we are often at war with one another. In a thousand little ways we demand to be catered to. We seldom esteem others as more important than ourselves. We often create strife by demanding our way rather than by walking in God's Spirit.

Leader: God blesses those who are persecuted because they live for God, for the Kingdom of Heaven is theirs.

People: But we have too often retreated from the disapproval of others. We've sought to please the world, rather than risking the disapproval of those who need the Messiah. We regard rejection for righteousness as a burden to be borne, rather than an honor to be humbly received.

Leader: Lord, please show us your mercy.

People: Lord, have mercy upon us in the name of the Father, Son, and Holy Spirit. Amen.

Leader: The proof of God's amazing love is this: while we were still sinners, Christ died for us. Because we have faith in him, we dare with confidence to approach him. Let us ask God to forgive us.

Unison: Almighty God, you love us through Christ, but we have not loved you; you call, but we have not always listened. We walked away from neighbors in time of need. God our Father, help us to face up to ourselves, so that, as you move toward us in mercy, we may repent, turn to you, and receive forgiveness; through Jesus Christ our Lord. Amen.

To you, O Lord, we lift up our souls. Make us to know your ways, O Lord; teach us your paths. Lead us in your truth, and teach us, for you are the God of our salvation; for you we wait all day long. Be mindful of your mercy, O Lord, and of your steadfast love, for they have existed from eternity. Remember not the sins of our youth, or our transgressions; according to your steadfast love remember us. For your name's sake, O Lord, pardon our great guilt. Turn toward us and be gracious, for we are lonely and afflicted. Relieve the troubles of our hearts, and bring us out of our distresses. Consider our affliction and our trouble, and forgive all our sins through Christ. Amen (From Psalm 25:1, 4–7, 11, 16–18).

Dear Father, we are thankful that your mercy is higher than the heavens, wider than our wanderings, deeper than all our sin. Forgive our frivolous attitude toward life, our callousness toward suffering, our envy of those who have more than we have, our obsession with creating a life of constant pleasure, our indifference to the treasure of heaven, our neglect of your wise and gracious law. Help us to change our way of life so that we may desire what is good, love what you love, and do what you command. Through Christ our Lord. Amen.

✝ Assurances of God's Forgiving Grace

Hear the good news! This statement is completely reliable and should be universally accepted: Christ Jesus entered the world to rescue sinners. He personally bore our sins in his body on the cross, so that we might be dead to sin and be alive to all that is good.

Who is in a position to condemn? Only Christ, and Christ died for us. Christ rose for us, Christ reigns in power for us, Christ prays for us. If a man is in Christ, he becomes a new person altogether—the past is finished and gone, everything has become fresh and new.

Leader: Friends, believe the good news of the gospel.
People: In Jesus Christ, we are forgiven.

"The LORD is merciful and gracious, slow to anger and abounding in steadfast love. He does not deal with us according to our sins, nor requite us according to our iniquities. For as the heavens are high above the earth, so great is his steadfast love toward those who fear him; as far as the east is from the west, so far does he remove our transgressions from us" (Psalm 103:8, 10–12 RSV).

"With everlasting love I will have compassion on you, says the LORD, your Redeemer. I am he who blots out your transgressions for my own sake, and I will not remember your sins. Return to me, for I have redeemed you" (Isaiah 54:8, 43:25, 44:22 NRSV). Believe this Gospel and go forth to live in peace. Amen.

"If God is for us, who is against us? He who did not spare his own Son but gave him up for us all, will he not also give us all things with him? Who shall bring any charge against God's elect? It is God who justifies, who is to condemn?" (Romans 8:31–34a RSV).

If we say we have no sin, we deceive ourselves, and the truth is not in us. If we confess our sins, he is faithful and just, and will forgive our sins and cleanse us from all unrighteousness.

"If anyone does sin, we have an advocate with the Father, Jesus Christ the righteous; and he is the atoning sacrifice for our sins, and not for ours only but also for the sins of the whole world" (1 John 2:1–2 NRSV).

Hear the gracious words of our Lord Jesus Christ to all who truly repent and turn to him. Come unto me, all you who labor and are heavy-laden, and I will give you rest. Him that comes to me I will never cast out. The grace of our Lord Jesus Christ be with you. Amen.

Almighty God, who doth freely pardon all who repent and turn to him, now fulfill in every contrite heart the promise of redeeming grace; remitting all our sins, and cleansing us from an evil conscience, through the perfect sacrifice of Christ Jesus our Lord. Amen.

"Surely he took up our infirmities and carried our sorrows, yet we considered him stricken by God, smitten by him, and afflicted. But he was pierced for our transgressions, he was crushed for our iniquities; the punishment that brought us peace was upon him, and by his wounds we are healed" (Isaiah 53:4–5).

To him who loves us and has freed us from our sins by his blood, and has made us to be a kingdom and priests to serve his God and Father—to him be glory and power for ever and ever! Amen.

✝ Prayers for Illumination

Almighty and gracious Father, since our whole salvation standeth in our knowledge of thy Holy Word, strengthen us now by thy Holy Spirit that our hearts may be set free from all worldly thoughts and attachments of the flesh, so that we may hear and receive that same Word, and, recognizing thy gracious will for us, may love and serve thee with earnest delight, praising and glorifying thee in Jesus Christ our Lord. Amen (John Calvin, derived from Martin Bucer, quoted in Bard Thompson, *Liturgies of the Western Church*, p. 209).

Almighty God, who has spoken to us through your Son, let your written Word now be spoken and heard by each of us. Give us ears to hear and hearts to understand, that we not refuse your calling or ignore your voice. May we all be taught by you through your powerful Word. Bring our every thought captive to obeying Christ, to the glory of your holy name. Amen.

Lord God, we acknowledge that your Word is full of living power. It is sharper than the sharpest knife, cutting deep into our innermost thoughts and desires. Your Word exposes us for what we really are. So with great awe and humility we bow before your Word. Speak to us, convict us, cleanse us, and equip us to obey your will. This we ask in the name of Jesus Christ. Amen.

We bow in your presence, Lord, acknowledging that all Scripture is inspired by you and is useful to teach us what is true and to make us realize what is wrong in our lives. It straightens us out and teaches us to do what is right. It is your way of preparing us in every way, equipped for every good thing you want us to do. May the reading and preaching of your inspired Word now accomplish your intended purposes as we wait on you, through Christ. Amen.

O great and glorious God, have the last word again today. We defer to your wisdom. Your counsels are eternally consistent. Your thoughts do not assume a new drift with each passing Sunday or with each passing generation. Set the agenda for your preached word, and control the lips of your servant. In Jesus' name. Amen. (© 1981, *Service Book*, CRC Publications, 2850 Kalamazoo SE, Grand Rapids, MI 49560. All rights reserved. Used by permission.)

✝ Offertory Prayers

Almighty God, the source of every good and perfect gift, accept the offerings which your people now present to you with willing and thankful hearts. Grant us the grace to set ourselves apart to your service, that we may glorify you this week and on into your heavenly kingdom. Through Jesus Christ our Lord. Amen.

Father of mercies, who gave your beloved Son for the life of your people, and has given us all things richly to enjoy, help us as we present our tithes and offerings to do so with thankfulness, and to present ourselves for your service. Through Jesus Christ our Lord. Amen.

Lord God, from whom we receive both our gifts and the power to give, grant that these offerings which we now bring to you may be used for your glory, through Jesus Christ our Lord. Amen.

Can it be said enough, Father, how blessed we are by your hands? Blessed today, and blessed immensely! In the light of that immense blessing, we must ask: What is the true measure of our wealth? What is prosperity? What is pleasure? What is it to be rich?

Prosperity is to know you. Pleasure is to please you. To be rich is to be bought by the blood of him who became poor that by his poverty we might become wealthy beyond measure.

So we gladly share today, Father. And we thank you for the privilege. In Jesus' name. Amen. (© 1981, *Service Book*, CRC Publications, 2850 Kalamazoo SE, Grand Rapids, MI 49560. All rights reserved. Used by permission.)

All that we have is from you, heavenly Father, for you are the Creator and preserver of all people and things. Accept these gifts we now bring in your presence. Help us to make our whole life an offering before you. We desire to seal this our worship in a renewed dedication of ourselves and our gifts and our time to your service. This we pray through Jesus Christ our Lord. Amen.

✝ Benedictions

"May the LORD bless you and protect you. May the LORD smile on you and be gracious to you. May the LORD show you his favor and give you his peace"

(Numbers 6:24–26 NLT). In the name of the Father, Son, and Holy Spirit. Amen.

"May the grace of our Lord Jesus Christ, the love of God, and the fellowship of the Holy Spirit be with you all. Amen" (2 Corinthians 13:13 NLT).

"May the God of peace, who brought again from the dead our Lord Jesus, equip you with all you need for doing his will. May he produce in you, through the power of Jesus Christ, all that is pleasing to him. Jesus is the great Shepherd of the sheep by an everlasting covenant, signed with his blood. To him be glory forever and ever. Amen" (Hebrews 13:20–21 NLT).

The blessing of God Almighty, the Father, the Son, and the Holy Spirit, be with all of you evermore. Amen.

May the God of hope fill you with all joy and peace in believing. May you overflow with hope through the power of the Holy Spirit, in the name of the triune God. Amen.

The peace of God, which passes all understanding, keep your hearts and minds in the knowledge and love of God, and of His Son Jesus Christ our Lord; and the blessings of God Almighty, the Father, the Son, and the Holy Spirit, be on, and remain with you always. Amen.

2

Doxologies

✝ Scriptural Doxologies

Luke 2:14 "Glory to God in the highest, and on earth peace to men on whom his favor rests."

Romans 9:5 "Christ, who is God over all, forever praised! Amen."

Romans 11:33–36 "Oh, the depth of the riches of the wisdom and knowledge of God! How unsearchable his judgments, and his paths beyond tracing out! Who has known the mind of the Lord? Or who has been his counselor? Who has ever given to God, that God should repay him? For from him and through him and to him are all things. To him be the glory forever! Amen."

Romans 16:27 "To the only wise God be glory forever through Jesus Christ! Amen."

Ephesians 3:20–21 "Now to him who is able to do immeasurably more than all we ask or imagine, according to his power that is at work within us, to him be glory in the church and in Christ Jesus throughout all generations, forever and ever! Amen."

Philippians 4:20 "To our God and Father be glory for ever and ever. Amen."

1 Timothy 1:17 "Now to the King eternal, immortal, invisible, the only God, be honor and glory for ever and ever. Amen."

1 Timothy 6:15–16 "God, the blessed and only Ruler, the King of kings and Lord of lords, who alone is immortal and who lives in unapproachable light, whom no one has seen or can see. To him be honor and might forever. Amen."

1 Peter 4:11 "If anyone serves, he should do it with the strength God provides, so that in all things God may be praised through Jesus Christ. To him be the glory and the power for ever and ever. Amen."

2 Peter 3:18 "But grow in the grace and knowledge of our Lord and Savior Jesus Christ. To him be glory both now and forever! Amen."

Jude 24–25 "To him who is able to keep you from falling and to present you before his glorious presence without fault and with great joy—to the only God our Savior be glory, majesty, power and authority, through Jesus Christ our Lord, before all ages, now and forevermore! Amen."

Revelation 5:13 "To him who sits on the throne and to the Lamb be praise and honor and glory and power, for ever and ever!"

Revelation 7:12 "Amen! Praise and glory and wisdom and thanks and honor and power and strength be to our God for ever and ever. Amen!"

✝ Musical Doxologies

Each doxology below includes the meter to which it is written. Look up the meter in the metrical index of a hymnal to find musical tunes to which the doxology may be sung.

To God the Father, God the Son,
And God the Spirit, praise be given,
The everlasting Three in One,
Adored by all in earth and heaven;
As was in circling ages past,
Is now, and shall forever be,
While saints their crowns of glory cast
Before your throne, blest Trinity. Amen. (LMD)

To praise the Father, and the Son,
And Spirit all-divine,
The One in Three, and Three in One
Let saints and angels join:
Glory to Thee, blest Three in One,
The God Whom we adore,
As was, and is, and shall be done,
When time shall be no more. Amen. (CMD)

Praise and honor to the Father,
Praise and honor to the Son,

Praise and honor to the Spirit,
Ever Three and ever One:
One in might and one in glory
While eternal ages run. Amen. (8.7.8.7.8.7)

Great Jehovah! we adore You,
God the Father, God the Son,
God the Spirit, joined in glory
On the same eternal throne:
Endless praises
To Jehovah, Three in One. Amen. (8.7.8.7.4.7)

Come, let us adore him, come, bow at His feet!
Oh! give him the glory, the praise that is meet!
Let joyful hosannas unceasing arise,
And join the full chorus that gladdens the skies!
    Amen. (11.11.11.11)

Praise God from whom all blessings flow;
Praise him, all creatures here below:
Alleluia, Alleluia!
Praise him above, ye heav'nly host;
Praise Father, Son, and Holy Ghost:
Alleluia, Alleluia, Alleluia,
Alleluia, Alleluia! (8.8.4.4.8.8 All Creatures of Our
    God and King)

Te Deum

You are God: we praise you;
You are the Lord: we acclaim you;
You are the eternal Father:
All creation worships you.
To you all angels, all the powers of heaven,
Cherubim and Seraphim, sing in endless praise:

Holy, holy, holy Lord, God of power and might,
heaven and earth are full of your glory.
The glorious company of apostles praise you.
The noble fellowship of prophets praise you.
The white-robed army of martyrs praise you.
Throughout the world the holy Church acclaims
you;
Father, of majesty unbounded,
your true and only Son, worthy of all worship,
and the Holy Spirit, advocate and guide.
You, Christ, are the king of glory,
the eternal Son of the Father.
When you became man to set us free
you did not shun the Virgin's womb.
You overcame the sting of death
and opened the kingdom of heaven to all believers.
You are seated at God's right hand in glory.
We believe that you will come and be our judge.
Come then, Lord, and help your people,
bought with the price of your own blood,
and bring us with your saints
to glory everlasting.

(*Book of Common Prayer,* 1979)

3

Affirmations of Faith

✝ Historic Affirmations

Apostles' Creed

I believe in God, the Father almighty,
    creator of heaven and earth.
I believe in Jesus Christ, God's only Son, our Lord;
    who was conceived by the Holy Spirit,
    born of the virgin Mary,
    suffered under Pontius Pilate,
    was crucified, died, and was buried;
    he descended to the dead.
    On the third day he rose again;
    he ascended into heaven,
    he is seated at the right hand of the Father,
    and he will come again to judge the living
        and the dead.
I believe in the Holy Spirit,
    the holy catholic church,
    the communion of saints,
    the forgiveness of sins,
    the resurrection of the body,
    and the life everlasting. Amen.

Musical Version of the Apostles' Creed
(tune: Ode to Joy)

> I believe in God the Father,
> Maker of the heaven and earth;
> And in Jesus Christ, our Savior,
> God's own Son, of matchless worth;
> By the Holy Ghost conceived,
> Virgin Mary bore God's Son,
> He, in whom I have believed,
> God Almighty, Three in One.
>
> Suffered under Pontius Pilate,
> Crucified, for me he died;
> Laid within a grave so silent,
> Gate of hell he opened wide;
> And the stone-sealed tomb was empty,
> On the third day he arose;
> Into heaven made his entry,
> Mighty conqueror of his foes.
>
> At God's right hand he is seated,
> Till his coming, as he said;
> Final judgment will be meted
> To the living and the dead.
> I confess the Holy Spirit
> Has been sent through Christ the Son;
> To apply salvation's merit,
> God the Spirit—Three in One.
>
> I believe the church of Jesus,
> Holy, catholic remains;
> We are one through all the ages,
> With communion of the saints.

I believe sins are forgiven,
That our bodies will be raised;
Everlasting life in heaven,
Amen, let his name be praised!

Responsive Version of the Apostles' Creed

Leader: In the presence of the Lord, the members of his church, and the onlooking angelic host, confess your beliefs.

Congregation: I believe in God the Father . . .

Leader: And declare your convictions concerning his Son.

Congregation: I believe in Jesus Christ . . .

Leader: Do you believe in the third person of the Trinity?

Congregation: I believe in the Holy Spirit . . .

Leader: And what do you believe about the future?

Congregation: I believe in the resurrection of the body and the life everlasting.

Leader: Amen.

Congregation: Amen.

The Apostles' Creed for Children

I believe God made the world, the sky, the stars, the animals, and all the people in the world.

I believe that God's Son, Jesus, came into the world from heaven. That's what we remember on Christmas. I believe Jesus died on the cross for my sins, for all the wrong things I do. But three days after he died, he became alive again. And he went into heaven, and now he is sitting by his heavenly Father again. I believe that someday soon he is going to come back to the world and I will see him.

I believe the Holy Spirit, who is God, lives inside me when Jesus is my Savior. I believe that God loves the people in my church and that he wants me to love them too. I believe that God forgives me of all the wrong, sinful things I do, because Jesus died for me. But God doesn't want me to keep doing what is wrong and sinful. I believe that someday I will live with God forever in heaven in my brand-new body!

I love you, Jesus, because you loved me first.

Gordon Terpstra, from *The Banner*, Grand Rapids, Michigan, February 9, 1987. Used with permission of *The Banner*, CRC Publications, Grand Rapids, MI 49560. All rights reserved.

The Nicene Creed

We believe in one God, the Father, the Almighty,
    maker of heaven and earth, of all that is, seen
        and unseen.
We believe in our Lord Jesus Christ,
    the only Son of God,
    eternally begotten of the Father,
    God from God, Light from Light,
        true God from true God,
    begotten, not made, of one Being with the Father;
    through him all things were made.
For us and for our salvation
    he came down from heaven,
    was incarnate of the Holy Spirit and the virgin Mary
    and became truly human.

For our sake he was crucified under Pontius Pilate;
he suffered death and was buried.
On the third day he rose again
    in accordance with the Scriptures;
he ascended into heaven and is seated
    at the right hand of the Father.
He will come again in glory
    to judge the living and the dead,
and his kingdom will have no end.
We believe in the Holy Spirit, the Lord,
    the giver of life,
    who proceeds from the Father and the Son,
    who with the Father and the Son is worshiped
      and glorified
    who has spoken through the prophets.
We believe in one holy catholic and apostolic church.
We acknowledge one baptism
    for the forgiveness of sins.
We look for the resurrection of the dead,
    and the life of the world to come. Amen.

Creedal Form from the Westminster Standards

I believe man's chief purpose is to glorify God, and to enjoy him forever.

I believe God is a Spirit, infinite, eternal and unchangeable, in his being, wisdom, power, holiness, justice, goodness, and truth; I believe there is but one true and living God; that there are three persons in the Godhead: the Father, the Son, and the Holy Spirit; and that these three are one God, the same in substance, equal in power and glory; I believe God has foreordained whatever comes to pass; that God made all things of nothing, by the word of his power, in the space of six days, and all very good; and that God preserves and governs all his creatures and all their actions.

I believe our first parents, though created in knowledge, righteousness, and holiness, sinned against God, by eating the forbidden fruit; and that their fall brought mankind into an estate of sin and misery; I believe God determined, out of his mere good pleasure, to deliver his elect out of the estate of sin and misery, and to bring them into an estate of salvation by a Redeemer; I believe the only Redeemer of God's elect is the Lord Jesus Christ, who, being the eternal Son of God, became man, and so was, and continues to be, God and man in two distinct natures, and one person, forever; I believe Christ, as our Redeemer, executes the office of a prophet, of a priest, and of a king. I believe Christ as our Redeemer underwent the miseries of this life, the wrath of God, the cursed death of the cross, and burial; He rose again from the dead on the third day, ascended up into heaven, sits at the right hand of God, the Father, and is coming to judge the world at the last day.

Adapted from a longer form in *Leading in Worship*, Terry L. Johnson, editor (Oak Ridge, Tennessee: The Covenant Foundation, 1996), p. 174. Used with permission.

From the Heidelburg Catechism
Leader: What is your only comfort in life and in death?
Congregation: That I am not my own,

but belong—
   body and soul,
   in life and in death—
to my faithful Savior Jesus Christ.

He has fully paid for all my sins with his precious
      blood,
and has set me free from the tyranny of the devil.
He also watches over me in such a way
that not a hair can fall from my head
without the will of my Father in heaven:
in fact, all things must work together for my
      salvation.

Because I belong to him,
Christ, by his Holy Spirit,
assures me of eternal life
and makes me whole-heartedly willing and ready
from now on to live for him.

From the Lausanne Covenant

1. We affirm our belief in the one-eternal God, Creator and Lord of the world, Father, Son and Holy Spirit, who governs all things according to the purpose of his will. He has been calling out from the world a people for himself, and sending his people back into the world to be his servants and his witnesses, for the extension of his kingdom, the building up of Christ's body, and the glory of his name. We confess with shame that we have often denied our calling and failed in our mission, by becoming con-

formed to the world or by withdrawing from it. Yet we rejoice that even when borne by earthen vessels the gospel is still a precious treasure. To that task of making that treasure known in the power of the Holy Spirit we desire to dedicate ourselves anew.

2. We affirm the divine inspiration, truthfulness and authority of both Old and New Testament Scriptures in their entirety as the only written Word of God, without error in all that it affirms, and the only infallible rule of faith and practice. We also affirm the power of God's Word to accomplish his purpose of salvation. The message of the Bible is addressed to all mankind. For God's revelation in Christ and in Scripture is unchangeable. Through it the Holy Spirit still speaks today. He illumines the minds of God's people in every culture to perceive its truth freshly through their own eyes and thus discloses to the whole church ever more of the many-colored wisdom of God.

✝ Biblical Affirmations

We believe "that Christ died for our sins according to the Scriptures, that he was buried, that he was raised on the third day according to the Scriptures, and that he appeared to Peter, and then to the Twelve. After that, he appeared to more than five hundred of the brothers at the same time" (1 Corinthians 15:3–6a).

We believe that Christ is Lord "who through the Spirit of holiness was declared with power to be the

45

Son of God by his resurrection from the dead: Jesus Christ our Lord" (Romans 1:3–4).

We "believe in him who raised Jesus our Lord from the dead. He was delivered over to death for our sins and was raised to life for our justification. Therefore, since we have been justified through faith, we have peace with God through our Lord Jesus Christ, through whom we have gained access by faith into this grace in which we now stand" (Romans 4:24–5:2a).

We believe that "Christ Jesus, who died—more than that, who was raised to life—is at the right hand of God and is also interceding for us" (Romans 8:34).

We confess our allegiance to Christ Jesus, "who, being in very nature God, did not consider equality with God something to be grasped, but made himself nothing, taking the very nature of a servant, being made in human likeness. And being found in appearance as a man, he humbled himself and became obedient to death—even death on a cross! Therefore God exalted him to the highest place and gave him the name that is above every name, that at the name of Jesus every knee should bow, in heaven and on earth and under the earth, and every tongue confess that Jesus Christ is Lord, to the glory of God the Father" (Philippians 2:6–11).

We confess belief in Jesus Christ our Lord. "He appeared in a body, was vindicated by the Spirit, was seen by angels, was preached among the nations, was believed on in the world, was taken up in glory" (1 Timothy 3:16).

We confess that "Christ also suffered when he died for our sins once for all time. He never sinned, but he died for sinners that he might bring us safely home to God. He suffered physical death, but he was raised to life in the Spirit. So he went and preached to the spirits in prison—those who disobeyed God long ago when God waited patiently while Noah was building his boat. Only eight people were saved from drowning in that terrible flood. And this is a picture of baptism, which now saves you by the power of Jesus Christ's resurrection. Baptism is not a removal of dirt from your body; it is an appeal to God from a clean conscience. Now Christ has gone to heaven. He is seated in the place of honor next to God, and all the angels and authorities and powers are bowing before him" (1 Peter 3:18–22 NLT).

We believe there is no condemnation for those who are in Christ Jesus: and we know that in everything God works for good with those who love him, who are called according to his purpose. We are sure that neither death, nor life, nor angels, nor principalities, nor things present, nor things to come, nor powers, nor height, nor depth, nor anything else in all creation, will be able to separate us from the love of God in Christ Jesus our Lord. Amen (Romans 8:1, 28, 38, 39, author's paraphrase).

This is the good news which we received, in which we stand, and by which we are saved: that Christ died

47

for our sins according to the Scriptures, that he was buried, that he was raised on the third day; and that he appeared to Peter, then to the Twelve, and to many faithful witnesses.

We believe he is the Christ, the Son of the living God. He is the first and the last, the beginning and the end; he is our Lord and our God. Amen (1 Corinthians 15:3–6; Revelation 22:13, author's paraphrase).

4

Offering Resources

✝ Offertory Verses

1 Chronicles 29:9 "The people rejoiced at the willing response of their leaders, for they had given freely and wholeheartedly to the LORD."

1 Chronicles 29:10b–14 "O LORD, the God of our ancestor Israel, may you be praised forever and ever! Yours, O LORD, is the greatness, the power, the glory, the victory, and the majesty. Everything in the heavens and on earth is yours, O LORD, and this is your kingdom. We adore you as the one who is over all things. Riches and honor come from you alone, for you rule over everything. Power and might are in your hand, and it is at your discretion that people are made great and given strength. O our God, we thank you and praise your glorious name! But who am I, and who are my people, that we could give anything to you? Everything we have has come from you, and we give you only what you have already given us!" (NLT).

Psalm 96:8 "Ascribe to the Lord the glory due his name; bring an offering and come into his courts."

Proverbs 3:9 "Honor the Lord with your wealth, with the firstfruits of all your crops."

Malachi 3:10 "Bring all the tithes into the storehouse so there will be enough food in my Temple. If you do," says the Lord Almighty, "I will open the windows of heaven for you. I will pour out a blessing so great you won't have enough room to take it in! Try it! Let me prove it to you!" (NLT).

Matthew 2:11 "They bowed down and worshiped him. Then they opened their treasures and presented him with gifts of gold and of incense and of myrrh."

Matthew 6:19–21 "Don't store up treasures here on earth, where they can be eaten by moths and get rusty, and where thieves break in and steal. Store your treasures in heaven, where they will never become moth-eaten or rusty and where they will be safe from thieves. Wherever your treasure is, there your heart and thoughts will also be" (NLT).

Matthew 6:31–33 "Do not worry, saying, 'What shall we eat?' or 'What shall we drink?' or 'What shall we wear?' For the pagans run after all these things, and your heavenly Father knows that you need them. But seek first his kingdom and his righteousness, and all these things will be given to you as well."

Luke 12:15 "Watch out! Be on your guard against all kinds of greed; a man's life does not consist in the abundance of his possessions."

Luke 16:13 "No servant can serve two masters. Either he will hate the one and love the other, or he will be devoted to the one and despise the other. You cannot serve both God and Money."

Acts 20:35b "Remembering the words the Lord Jesus himself said: 'It is more blessed to give than to receive.'"

Romans 12:1 "Therefore, I urge you, brothers, in view of God's mercy, to offer yourselves as living sacrifices, holy and pleasing to God—which is your spiritual worship."

1 Corinthians 16:2 "On the first day of every week, each one of you should set aside a sum of money in keeping with his income."

2 Corinthians 8:3–5 "For I can testify that they gave not only what they could afford but far more. And they did it of their own free will. They begged us again and again for the gracious privilege of sharing in the gift for the Christians in Jerusalem. Best of all, they went beyond our highest hopes, for their first action was to dedicate themselves to the Lord and to us for whatever directions God might give them" (NLT).

2 Corinthians 8:9 "You know the grace of our Lord Jesus Christ, that though he was rich, yet for your sakes he became poor, so that you through his poverty might become rich."

2 Corinthians 8:12 "If you are really eager to give, it isn't important how much you are able to give. God wants you to give what you have, not what you don't have" (NLT).

2 Corinthians 9:6–7 "Remember this—a farmer who plants only a few seeds will get a small crop. But the one who plants generously will get a generous crop. You must each make up your own mind as to how much you should give. Don't give reluctantly or in response to pressure. For God loves the person who gives cheerfully" (NLT).

2 Corinthians 9:8 "God is able to make all grace abound to you, so that in all things at all times, having all that you need, you will abound in every good work."

2 Corinthians 9:10–11 "For God is the one who gives seed to the farmer and then bread to eat. In the same way, he will give you many opportunities to do good, and he will produce a great harvest of generosity in you" (NLT).

2 Corinthians 9:12–14 "This service that you perform is not only supplying the needs of God's people but is also overflowing in many expressions of thanks to God. Because of the service by which you have proved yourselves, men will praise God for the obedience that accompanies your confession of the gospel of Christ, and for your generosity in sharing with them and with everyone else. And in their prayers for you their hearts will go out to you, because of the surpassing grace God has given you."

2 Corinthians 9:15 "Thank God for his Son—a gift too wonderful for words!" (NLT).

Philippians 4:18b–19 "They are a sweet-smelling sacrifice that is acceptable to God and pleases him. And this same God who takes care of me will supply all your needs from his glorious riches, which have been given to us in Christ Jesus" (NLT).

Hebrews 13:16 "Do not forget to do good and to share with others, for with such sacrifices God is pleased."

James 1:17 "Every good and perfect gift is from above, coming down from the Father of the heavenly lights, who does not change like shifting shadows."

✝ Offertory Responses

Leader: Watch out! Be on your guard against all kinds of greed; a man's life does not consist in the abundance of his possessions.

People: No servant can serve two masters. Either he will hate the one and love the other, or he will be devoted to the one and despise the other. You cannot serve both God and Money.

Leader: Therefore, I urge you, in view of God's mercy, to offer yourselves as living sacrifices, holy and pleasing to God—which is your spiritual worship.

People: We do not want to forget to do good and to share with others, for with such sacrifices God is pleased.

Leader: May the gifts we now offer be a fragrant offering, an acceptable sacrifice, pleasing to God.

Leader: Whoever sows sparingly will also reap sparingly, and whoever sows generously will also reap generously. Each person should give what he has decided in his heart to give, not reluctantly or under compulsion, for God loves a cheerful giver.

People: May our gifts be a fragrant offering, an acceptable sacrifice, pleasing to God.

Leader: And my God will meet all your needs according to his glorious riches in Christ Jesus.

People: We do not want to forget to do good and to share with others, for with such sacrifices God is pleased.

As the forgiven and redeemed people of God, let us offer to him ourselves and our gifts.

With joyful hearts, let us now present the offering of our lives and our labors from this week to our Lord.

✝ Offering Songs

Praise God from whom all blessings flow;
Lift praise, all creatures here below:
Alleluia, Alleluia!
Praise him above, you heav'nly host;
Praise Father, Son, and Holy Ghost:
Alleluia, Alleluia, Alleluia,
Alleluia, Alleluia.

Tune: All Creatures
of Our God and King

All things are yours: no gift have we,
Lord of all gifts, to offer thee;
And hence with thankful hearts today,
your own before your feet we lay.

Tune: Germany

Give us, Lord, the grace of giving
With a spirit wide and free
That ourselves and all our living,
We may offer unto thee. Amen.

Tune: Stuttgart

5

Music Resources

 Five-Phase Hymns and Choruses

The following is a way to structure a time of singing following the progression used in Psalm 95. Choose one or more hymns or choruses from each of the five phases.

Invitation (Psalm 95:1)

We Bring the Sacrifice of Praise
Don't You Know It's Time to Praise the Lord
I Just Came to Praise the Lord
Let's Forget about Ourselves
Spirit Song
Come, Worship the Lord
As We Gather
This Is the Day That the Lord Has Made
Come, Christians Join to Sing
Praise the Savior, Ye Who Know Him
My Faith Has Found a Resting Place
Let's All Go up to Zion
Come, We That Love the Lord

Engagement (Psalm 95:2)

Our God Is an Awesome God
How Majestic
Rejoice in the Lord Always
He Is the King
Great and Mighty Is He
The Celebration Song
I Will Sing of the Mercies of the Lord
I Shall Prepare Him My Heart
O Worship the King
All Creatures of Our God and King
Guide Me, O Thou Great Jehovah
Come, Thou Almighty King
O for a Thousand Tongues to Sing

Exaltation (Psalm 95:3–5)

All the Earth Shall Worship
Let There Be Glory and Honor and Praises
All Hail King Jesus
We Exalt Thee
Our God Reigns
Thou Art Worthy
Majesty
I Just Want to Praise You
Crown Him with Many Crowns
Immortal, Invisible
Rejoice, the Lord Is King!
How Great Thou Art
All Hail the Power of Jesus' Name

Adoration (Psalm 95:6)

We Worship and Adore You
Glorify Your Name
His Name Is Wonderful
I Love You, Lord
Emmanuel
Lord, We Praise You
Father, I Adore You
Praise Song
Fairest Lord Jesus
My Jesus, I Love Thee
Be Thou My Vision
Jesus, Priceless Treasure
Majestic Sweetness Sits Enthroned
Of the Father's Love Begotten
How Sweet the Name of Jesus Sounds
He Hideth My Soul

Intimacy (Psalm 95:7)

O Lord, You're Beautiful
Turn Your Eyes upon Jesus
My Delight
Alleluia, Alleluia
As the Deer
Sweet Perfume
Holy Ground
In Moments Like These
Jesus, I Am Resting, Resting
Jesus, the Very Thought of Thee
Children of the Heavenly Father
Close to Thee

O to Be Like Thee!
Savior, Like a Shepherd
I Need Thee Every Hour
In the Garden

Closeout

We Are One in the Spirit
In My Life, Lord, Be Glorified
Holy, Holy, Holy
Shine, Jesus, Shine
He Is Able, More than Able
Thank You, Lord, for Saving My Soul
Our God Reigns
It Is Well
My Tribute
To God Be the Glory
And Can It Be
Our Great Savior
May the Mind
Fairest Lord Jesus
Great Is Thy Faithfulness
Because He Lives

Adapted from *The New Worship* by Barry Liesch (Grand Rapids: Baker Books, 1996), pp. 58–59.

 # Contemporary Orders of Worship

The following are examples of orders of worship used in some churches which employ contemporary worship. The songs are examples of what might be used.

Order 1 (Five-Phase Set with Choruses and Hymns)

Invitation (Stand)
 We Bring the Sacrifice of Praise
 He Has Made Me Glad
Engagement
 Rejoice in the Lord Always
Exaltation
 Rejoice, the Lord Is King!
 Crown Him with Many Crowns
Exaltation/Adoration (Sit)
 Glorify Your Name
Adoration
 I Love You, Lord
Intimacy
 As the Deer
Closeout (Stand)
 Fairest Lord Jesus
Time of Prayer
Ministry of the Word
Closing and Dismissal

Order 2

Vocal Prelude
 Come and Sing Praises
 All Hail the Power
 Reprise—Come and Sing Praises
Prayer
Vocal Call to Worship
 Celebrate Jesus
 Jesus Is His Name

O for a Thousand Tongues (contemporary and
traditional)
Selection by Music/Worship Team
Be Magnified
We Will Glorify
Opportunity for Confession and Reflection
In Christ Alone
Worship with Offerings
Fellowship of Concerns and Announcements
Drama
Message of the Day
Dismissal Prayer

Order 3
Call to Worship
Welcome
Worship Choruses
Scripture Reading and Prayer Time
Musical Selection
Offering Gifts
Drama or Interview
Message
Musical Selection
Closing

Order 4—Convergence (Blended) Worship
Welcome
Announcements
Invocation
Processional
Opening Prayer
Ministry of Praise and Worship with Music

61

Worship through Readings and Responses
  Ministry of the Word Entrance
  Collect for the Day
  Old Testament Reading
  Psalm (may be sung)
  New Testament Reading from Epistles
  Hymn/Chorus
  Gospel Reading
The Ministry of the Word
  Sermon
  Response Invitation
  Affirmation of Faith
Prayers of the People
  Intercession
  Confession of Sin
  Mutual Greeting and Passing of Peace
  Offering
Holy Communion
  Prayer of Thanksgiving
  Administration of the Elements
Dismissal
  Words of Exhortation
  Benediction
  Dismissal Hymn/Song

Hymn Festival Ideas

Cycle of the Church Year Hymn Festival

Call to Worship

Invocation

Introduction to the Church Year *(Give an explanation of the cycle of the church year)*

Advent Hymn—O Come, O Come Emmanuel

The Season of Advent *(Give an explanation of the season)*

Advent Reading—Isaiah 40:1–5

The Season of Christmas

Christmas Hymn—Joy to the World

Christmas Reading—Matthew 1:18–25

The Season of Epiphany *(Give an explanation of the season)*

Epiphany Hymn—We Three Kings

Epiphany Reading—Matthew 2:1–11

Choral Selection

The Season of Lent *(Give an explanation of the season)*

Lenten Reading—Matthew 26:27–54

Lenten Hymn—O Sacred Head Now Wounded

Prayer

The Season of Easter

Easter Reading—Matthew 28:1-10

Easter Hymn—Christ the Lord Is Risen Today

The Season of Pentecost *(Give an explanation of the season)*

Pentecost Reading—Acts 2:1–8, 12–21

Pentecost Hymn—Spirit of God, Descend upon My Heart

Benediction

Church Music through History Hymn Festival

Prelude

Call to Worship

Invocation

Gloria Patri
Scripture Reading—Psalm 96
Early Church Music
    Hymn—O Come, O Come, Emmanuel (Latin, 9th century plainsong)
    Hymn—O Splendor of God's Glory Bright (St. Ambrose, 4th century)
Reformation Church Music
    Scripture Reading—Psalm 46
    Hymn—A Mighty Fortress Is Our God (Martin Luther, 1483–1546)
    Hymn—I Greet Thee, Who My Sure Redeemer Art (John Calvin, 1509–1564)
Seventeenth- and Eighteenth-Century English Music
    Hymn—When I Survey the Wondrous Cross (Isaac Watts, 1674–1748)
    Hymn—O for a Thousand Tongues (Charles Wesley, 1707–1788)
    Scripture Reading—Colossians 3:16–17
Gospel Music
    Hymn—Jesus, Keep Me Near the Cross (Fanny Crosby, 1820–1915)
    Hymn—What a Friend We Have in Jesus (Joseph Scriven, 1820–1866)
Contemporary Church Music
    Scripture Reading—Revelation 5
    Hymn—God of the Ages or Lord of the Universe (Margaret Clarkson, 1915–)
    Chorus—El Shaddai (Michael Card, 1957–)
    Chorus—Our God Reigns (Leonard W. Smith Jr., 1942–)
Benediction

6

Worship Themes
Acts of the Triune God

✝ **God's Act of Creation**

Call to Worship Texts

Genesis 1:1
2 Kings 19:15
Nehemiah 9:6
Psalm 24:1–2; 33:6–9; 95:1–6; 100:1–3;
   102:25–27; 104:24; 121:1–2; 136:3–9; 148:1–6
Jeremiah 51:15–16
Amos 4:13
Hebrews 1:10–12; 11:3
Revelation 4:11

Responsive Call to Worship

Leader: Come, let us sing for joy to the Lord. Come,
   let us bow down in worship, let us kneel before
   the Lord our Maker.

Men: It is by faith that our minds accept that the whole universe was formed by God's command;

Women: That the world which we see has come into being through what is invisible.

Leader: By the Word of the Lord were the heavens made, their starry host by the breath of his mouth.

Men: God also created man in his own image, in the image of God he created him.

Women: Male and female he created them. God saw all that he had made and it was very good.

Unison: You are worthy, O Lord our God, to receive glory and honor and power, for you created all things; by your will they existed and were created. All praise belongs to you, our Creator, for your works!

Prayer of Adoration

You are worthy, O Lord, and we have been drawn to assemble together this day in Christ's name. We come from a busy week to enter your presence in adoration. We acknowledge that in the beginning you spoke and caused the earth, sun, moon, and all forms of life to come into existence. You spoke and whole galaxies came into being. You spoke and created us male and female in your image.

We look at the world of nature around us and see your handiwork, which calls for praise to be directed to you. The colors and shapes and textures around us point to your creative care. The fragrances and tastes and sounds echo your creativity. How good and pleasant and fitting it is for us to come before you in praise this hour. Fill our hearts with the power of your indwelling Spirit to give you the worship of which you are supremely worthy. Stir our hearts in a fresh way to sing joyfully to you. Then send us forth at the end of the hour to glorify and enjoy you wherever we go this new week. We praise you through the name of Jesus Christ and with the help of the Holy Spirit. Amen.

God's Act of Election

Call to Worship Texts

Deuteronomy 7:6–8
Psalm 65:4
John 6:37, 39, 44; 15:16
Acts 13:48
Romans 8:29–30
Ephesians 1:3–5, 11–12; 2:10
2 Thessalonians 2:13
1 Peter 1:1–2
1 Peter 2:9

Responsive Call to Worship

Leader: Praise be to the God and Father of our Lord Jesus Christ, who has blessed us in the heavenly realms with every spiritual blessing in Christ. For he chose us in him before the creation of the world to be holy and blameless in his sight. In love he predestined us to be adopted as his sons and daughters through Jesus Christ, in accordance with his pleasure and will.

People: Therefore we praise your glorious grace, which you have freely given us in Christ whom you love and whom we worship this hour. We praise you for your sovereign and undeserved act of choosing.

Prayer of Adoration

Sovereign Lord, we humbly bow before your throne. You are the Shepherd and we are the sheep. You are the Potter and we are the clay. We come with a sense of awe and wonder that you would take the initiative in eternity past to choose us to receive the free gift of life eternal. We marvel that you reached out and chose us not on the basis of any pre-existing goodness in us, but purely according to the good pleasure of your will. We have no grounds for boasting but only cause to bow before your throne lost in wonder, love, and praise. We desire to worship you this day in preparation for eternity in which we will gather with the elect from all ages and nations to lift up homage before your throne. Accept now our worship as we humbly offer it in the name of your Son, our Savior, Jesus Christ. Amen.

Christ's Incarnation

Call to Worship Texts
Isaiah 7:14; 9:6
Micah 5:2
Luke 1:68–69; 2:10–13, 14
John 1:14
Galatians 4:4–5

Responsive Call to Worship

Leader: I bring you good news of great joy that will be for all the people. Today in the town of David a Savior has been born to you.

People: He is Christ the Lord!

Leader: We praise the God of grace saying,

People: Glory to God in the highest, and on earth peace to those on whom his favor rests.

Leader: Let us all worship him with all our heart, soul, mind, and strength proclaiming,

Unison: Thanks be to God for his indescribable gift! The incarnate Christ, Immanuel, has come among us!

Prayer of Adoration

Almighty God, our Father, we gather to celebrate the coming of your Son into our world. You caused this day to shine with the brightness of Jesus Christ, the light of the world. You gave to us the gift of your only-begotten Son to take our nature upon himself. He humbled himself to be born in the lowly town of Bethlehem in a lowly manger. We rejoice that you sent angelic messengers to announce the good news. You prepared shepherds to come and bow in wonder and awe at the miracle of the incarnation. We would join them around the manger to let you know how much we appreciate the great things you have done for us.

Father, we set aside the rush of holiday shopping, the responsibilities of our careers, and the details of family plans to come apart and meditate on what the birth of Christ means. We stand amazed that you would be willing to take the initiative to come to our planet to visit us.

Help us now to sing and pray with appreciative hearts. Open our eyes to see the light shining in the darkness. Open our hearts to receive the living Christ as our Savior. Fill us with the peace which he came to bring, the inner peace which surpasses human understanding. Help us then go forth knowing why this is special good news. This we pray in the name of the one whose birth we celebrate, even our Wonderful Counselor, Mighty God, Everlasting Father, and Prince of Peace. Amen.

Christ's Acts of Shepherding

Call to Worship Texts
Psalm 23; 95:1–7; 100
John 10:1–16
Hebrews 13:20–21

Responsive Call to Worship

Leader: Come, let us join our voices to worship our Lord Jesus Christ for his work of shepherding us as the Good Shepherd.

People: Because the Lord is our shepherd, we shall not want. He makes us to lie down in green pastures; he leads us beside the still waters.

Leader: He restores our soul; he leads us in the paths of righteousness for his name's sake.

People: Yea, though we walk through the valley of the shadow of death, we will fear no evil; for you are with us; your rod and your staff comfort us.

Leader: You prepare a table before us in the presence of our enemies; you anoint our head with oil; our cup overflows.

People: Surely goodness and mercy shall follow us all the days of our life; and we will dwell in the house of the Lord forever. All praise to the Shepherd and Guardian of our souls.

Prayer of Adoration

Father, we come to express our appreciation for you as our great Shepherd. We are your sheep whom you know by name. Accept now the praise we as your flock offer in your presence.

We thank you sincerely for your personal shepherding care. You have led us through green pastures and by still waters in the paths of righteousness. You have restored our soul in times of need, and comforted us with your rod and staff. You have not deserted us in times of danger—even in the valley of the shadow of death. You continually remain with us as our loving Shepherd when we drive on the highway, when we work at our jobs, when we relax at home, when we study in the classroom, and even when we travel out of town. How we appreciate your constant shepherding care. Thank you for reaching out when we wander from the path because of temptations, doubts, and discouragements.

Our hearts are full of thanksgiving as we worship through Christ our Chief Shepherd, the Great Shepherd of the sheep. Amen.

✝ Christ's Act of Redemption

Call to Worship Texts

Isaiah 53:4–6
Mark 10:45
Romans 3:23–26; 5:6–8
Hebrews 10:19–22
1 Peter 2:24; 3:18
Revelation 1:5–6; 5:9, 10, 12

Responsive Call to Worship

Leader: Let us join our voices to praise the spotless
Lamb, Jesus Christ, who has redeemed us from
sin and death.

Congregation: We, whom he has redeemed, will sing
praises and shout for joy this hour;

Leader: Because in Christ the Lamb we have redemption through his blood, the forgiveness of our
sins in accordance with the riches of his grace.

Congregation: Christ has redeemed us from the curse
of the law by becoming a curse for us.

Leader: Let us praise him saying,

Unison: Worthy is the Lamb, who was slain, to receive
power and wealth and wisdom and strength
and honor and glory and praise! To him who
sits on the throne and to the Lamb we give worship this hour and forever and ever. Amen.

Prayer of Adoration

We approach your throne this hour, O God of all
grace, with gratitude for the person and work of

Jesus Christ. We come to turn our eyes away from ourselves and on to him. We thank you for planning in eternity past to provide a means of redemption through the sending of your Son. You have provided an ample remedy for the alienation of sin. You have provided one who gave his life blood as our substitute. You enabled him to bear the wrath which we deserved for our disobedience. He willingly endured pain and suffering out of love for us and obedience to you. You made it possible for the blood of Christ to cover over our sins and remove their stain. You have freed us from the weight of guilt and from eternal condemnation. How can we help but love and adore you for the rest of our lives. You have made the ultimate sacrifice to redeem us.

So we come this hour to sing your perfections; to acknowledge what Christ has already accomplished on our behalf. Thank you that his work in past history continues to be efficacious in this century. We glory in the cross because without the cross we would be helplessly lost. We come today resting all our trust for forgiveness and eternal life in the person and work of Christ. Even in the future eternal kingdom we will sing the glories of being redeemed by the Lamb. Accept our worship this hour as we present it through Christ our Redeemer. Amen.

 ## Christ's Resurrection

Call to Worship Texts
Job 19:25
1 Corinthians 15:3, 4, 20

1 Peter 1:3
Revelation 1:4, 5, 17, 18

Responsive Call to Worship

Leader: Christ is risen.
People: He is risen indeed. Alleluia!
Leader: Praise the God and Father of our Lord Jesus Christ.
People: He has made us resurrection people by raising Jesus from the dead.
Leader: Rejoice, then, even in your distress.
People: We shall be counted worthy when Christ appears.
Leader: God has claimed us as his own.
People: He called us from our darkness into the light of his day.
Leader: Christ is risen.
People: He is risen indeed. Alleluia!

Prayer of Adoration

Our Father God, we come this Easter Day in the name of the living Christ, who has come among us in this sanctuary. We assemble on the day on which your power raised Christ after his atoning death for our sins. We assemble on the day on which your disciples saw the moved stone and empty tomb. We assemble on the same day in which your Son appeared to eyewitnesses in triumph over sin and death. How grateful we are to be part of the stream of believers who down through the generations have celebrated the resurrection.

Accept now the praise of this congregation. Blessed are you for granting us new birth to a living hope through the resurrection of Christ. He has opened to us the door to eternal life. We worship him who holds the keys to life and death and lives forevermore as our risen Lord at your right hand. We join the voices of cherubim and seraphim to ascribe honor to the One who has filled us with new life and hope.

Fill our hearts with rejoicing that spills over into the days beyond Easter. May resurrection life and power be evident in our lives because we know him who is the resurrection and the life. This we pray in Christ's name and for his glory. Amen.

Christ's Ascension

Call to Worship Texts
Psalm 24:7–10; 68:17–18
Luke 24:50–52
Acts 1:8–9
Romans 8:34
Ephesians 1:19–21
Colossians 3:1
1 Timothy 3:16
Hebrews 4:14–19
1 Peter 3:22

Responsive Call to Worship
Leader: Christ died and rose again that we might have eternal life.
Congregation: All thanks rightly belongs to Jesus.

Leader: This same Christ ascended to heaven.
Congregation: He ascended that we might experience
God's presence and power. All praise be to God
for the ascension.

Prayer of Adoration

Lord God Most High, we come acknowledging that
Jesus Christ died and rose again on the third day that
we might have eternal life. Forty days later he ascended
to heaven in order that we might experience God's presence and power. We give thanks that Christ's earthly
mission was completed in obedience to your will. We
are humbled that we can now approach your throne
through the intercession of Christ. Since we have been
raised with Christ, we desire to set our hearts on things
above, where Christ is seated at your right hand. Help
us to set our minds on heavenly, eternal realities as we
by faith ascend and participate in heavenly realities this
hour. Accept our worship and thanksgiving, which we
now offer through Christ in whose name we pray.
Amen.

God's Act of Sending the Holy Spirit at Pentecost

Call to Worship Texts

Joel 2:28–32
John 16:5–15
Acts 2:1–21
Ephesians 5:18–20

Responsive Call to Worship

Leader: This is the day which Jesus promised: You shall receive power when the Holy Spirit has come upon you, and you shall be my witnesses to the ends of the earth.

Women: God has poured out his love in our hearts by the Holy Spirit, whom he has given us.

Men: We know that we live in him and he in us, because he has given us of his Spirit.

Women: The Spirit of the Lord now fills the whole world.

Men: Shout for joy to the Lord, all the earth.

Unison: May the peoples of all nations of the earth praise you. Come, Holy Spirit, come among us this hour and refresh us that we might glorify the Lord!

Prayer of Adoration

Spirit of the living God, fall fresh on us today. We call on you through the name of Jesus Christ. Descend on our hearts in this sanctuary in a fresh way to empower us, to refresh us, to motivate us. How we need your presence to keep us from becoming cold, routine, and mechanical in our worship. How we need your vitality to enable us to sing joyfully. How we need your Spirit to comprehend and apply the truths of Scripture we'll hear this hour. Help us to enter enthusiastically into spirit-filled worship this Pentecost Sunday. Then send us forth from this service to live spirit-filled lives all this week. This we pray in the name of Christ by the power of the Spirit who is among us. Amen.

✝ Christ's Return

Call to Worship Texts

Psalm 96:11–13; 98:7–9
Daniel 7:13–14
Matthew 24:30–31
Mark 13:26–27
Acts 1:11
1 Thessalonians 4:16–17
Titus 2:11–13
Hebrews 9:27–28
James 5:8
2 Peter 3:10–13
Revelation 1:7; 22:12–13

Responsive Call to Worship

Leader: Christ, who has come the first time, has promised a second advent. Let us worship in anticipation of his fulfillment of that promise.

Unison: The Lord himself will come down from heaven, with a loud command, with the voice of the archangel and with the trumpet call of God, and the dead in Christ will rise first. After that, we who are still alive and left will be caught up with them in the clouds to meet the Lord in the air. We honor the Alpha and Omega, the First and the Last, the Beginning and the End. Amen. Come, Lord Jesus!

Prayer of Adoration

Our Lord and Savior, the only True God, we thank you that you have come among us just as you have promised. Along with millions of believers around the world this day, we lift our voices in praise. We join our voices with those of the angels and archangels and all the hosts of heaven above. Stir our hearts by the power of your Holy Spirit to express heartfelt worship for Jesus Christ. Fill us with anticipation for his glorious return in the clouds of the skies to usher us into the eternal kingdom of heaven. We anticipate gathering around the throne to continue to glorify and enjoy you forever.

We ask that you might cleanse us of any sins that would create barriers between us and you, or between us and any other brother or sister in Christ. Forgive us through the sacrifice of Christ the Lamb who now sits at your right hand and has opened the door for us to enter the heavenlies as forgiven sinners. We long for the return of Jesus Christ and now raise this prayer in his exalted name. Maranatha. Amen.

7

Worship Themes
Attributes of the Triune God

✝ **God Is Beautiful**

Call to Worship Texts
2 Chronicles 3:6; 20:21
Job 40:9–10
Psalm 8:1; 27:4; 29:1–2; 36:7; 90:17; 96:6; 145:5
Isaiah 35:2
Zechariah 9:16–17

Responsive Call to Worship

Leader: Let us lift our voices this hour to praise the triune God who is the source of all beauty in the world he has created and who is inherently beautiful in his being and character.

People: O Lord our God, how excellent is your name in all the earth. You have set your glory above the heavens.

Leader: We praise the beauty of your holiness.

People: You are surrounded with majesty and excellence. You are arrayed with glory and beauty.

Leader: How great is your beauty.

People: Open our eyes that we may see and appreciate your beauty.

Leader: Let the beauty of the Lord our God be upon us his bride.

Unison: One thing have we desired of you, that will we seek after—that we may dwell in your house all the days of our lives, to behold your beauty. We adore, praise, and honor you, the source and perfection of all that is beautiful. In the name of the Father, Son, and Holy Spirit. Amen.

Prayer of Adoration

Father God Most High, who are we as unworthy sinners to come into your presence? Yet you have made it possible for us to boldly approach your throne because of the perfect work and righteousness of Jesus Christ which has been credited to our account. We enter your presence because Christ has forgiven us and granted us access.

Lord, as we come before you we are overwhelmed at the awesome sight of your beauty. You are the perfect source of all beauty and the creator of all that is beautiful in the world of nature that surrounds us. You have given us senses by which we can learn to perceive and appreciate beauty. How we thank you for the beauty of sunsets, fields of wildflowers, snow-capped mountains, works of art on canvas, symphony orchestras, and words artfully expressed in prose and poetry.

But above all these, we pause to express appreciation for you, the source of everything that possesses beauty. To look on you is to gaze on unmeasured beauty. You are perfection at the highest level, the personification of absolute delight. Words cannot describe you because you are transcendently beautiful.

Therefore we join the psalmist in saying that our desire is to dwell in the house of the Lord all the days of our lives to behold your beauty. During this hour may your beauty rest upon us as we lift up adoration in your presence through Christ. Amen.

God Is Eternal

Call to Worship Texts

Deuteronomy 33:26–27
1 Chronicles 29:10
Nehemiah 9:5
Job 36:26
Psalm 33:11; 90:1–2, 4; 92:8; 93:2; 102:12, 24–27;
    135:13; 145:13
Isaiah 26:4; 40:28; 41:4; 44:6
Lamentations 5:19
1 Timothy 1:17
Hebrews 1:10–12
Revelation 1:8; 4:8; 22:13

Responsive Call to Worship

Leader: We have assembled this Sunday to praise the
    timelessly eternal one who is the first and the

last. Praise belongs to him from everlasting to everlasting. Before the mountains were born or he brought forth the earth and the world, from everlasting to everlasting, he is God. He remains the same and his years will never end.

Congregation: Let us praise the Alpha and the Omega, who is, and who was, and who is to come—Jesus Christ the same yesterday, today, and forever. We worship our Lord who transcends all finite time.

Prayer of Adoration

Our eternal Father, we call on you and enter your timeless presence through Jesus Christ, who is the same yesterday, and today, and forever. We pray that you will help us to focus our thoughts on you and on eternal realities this hour. We set aside this time on the first day of the week to express praise and thanksgiving to you. We pray for the supernatural ministry of the Holy Spirit to stir us to heartfelt praise and adoration. May we then leave this sanctuary with a fresh desire to invest time and possessions each day this week in ways that will count for eternity. For we pray this through the person and work of Christ Jesus. Amen.

✝ God Is Faithful

Call to Worship Texts

Deuteronomy 7:9
Psalm 36:5; 89:1, 2, 5, 8, 33; 92:1–2; 119:89–90
Isaiah 25:1
Lamentations 3:23

1 Corinthians 1:9
2 Timothy 2:11–13
Hebrews 10:19–23

Responsive Call to Worship

Leader: God who has called you into fellowship with his Son, Jesus Christ, our Lord, is faithful.

People: He is a faithful Lord, keeping his covenant of love to a thousand generations of those who love him and keep his commands.

Leader: His faithfulness reaches to the skies and continues throughout all generations on into eternity.

Unison: We therefore praise the faithfulness of our Lord Jesus Christ in this assembly saying, Great is your faithfulness! We will exalt and praise your name, for in perfect faithfulness you have done marvelous things. Great is your faithfulness to us, O Lord our God.

Prayer of Adoration

God of all grace, you who have called us into fellowship with Christ, are faithful. So we come this Sunday to honor you for the essential quality of your character which means so much to us. We rest with confidence on you and your Word—knowing that you are totally trustworthy.

How faithful you have been in sustaining the world of nature around us which we enjoy. You faithfully send sunshine and rain, day and night, winter and summer, spring and fall. You have been so faithful in meeting our physical and temporal needs.

At the same time we thank you for establishing your covenant whereby we can come to know you through your faithful Son Jesus Christ. Even when we are unfaithful, we know that you remain faithful to forgive our sins as we confess and repent before you. In the midst of temptations which would pull us away from you, you remain faithful in providing a way out, so we can bear up under it. You have given us so many promises which you have faithfully kept and will keep on into eternity. You are never less than faithful, never unreliable. The thought of this fills our hearts to overflowing with love for you.

In response to your faithfulness stir our hearts in worship this hour. Stir our wills to be faithful to you all through this new week. This we pray in the name of our faithful Savior and Lord, Jesus Christ, through whom we offer all our praise this hour. Amen.

 God Is Good

Call to Worship Texts

2 Chronicles 5:13–14

Psalm 25:8; 34:8; 86:5; 100:4–5; 106:1; 107:1; 118:1, 29; 136:1; 145:7–9

Lamentations 3:25

Nahum 1:7

Romans 11:22

James 1:17

Responsive Call to Worship

Leader: Praise be to the God and Father of our Lord Jesus Christ,

People: Who has blessed us in the heavenly realms with every spiritual blessing in Christ.

Leader: He who did not spare his own Son, but gave him up for us all—how will he not also, along with him, graciously give us all things?

People: Everything he created is good.

Leader: We acknowledge that every good and perfect gift is from above.

People: So we present our worship this day to the One who is good and a generous gift-giver. Thanks be to the Father, Son, and Holy Spirit for all the good and perfect gifts which he continues to give us. We exalt you in this assembly!

Prayer of Adoration

Our Father God, the Blessed and only Ruler, we gather with thanks this Sunday. How grateful we are for the good and generous gifts you have given to us. We come both young and old, male and female, to honor you—the ultimate source of goodness and the source of every good and perfect gift.

Thank you for your acts of creation by which you formed the earth and all it contains out of nothing. How appropriate that you pronounced it all good upon completion. We have enjoyed your good earthly gifts this week—including the tasty and nourishing food which we have enjoyed from your hand. We thank you for the beauty of the seasons including the splendor of colors in the fall and the first signs of new life in the spring.

Thank you for your acts of goodness in giving us friends and families with whom we can share your gifts. By common grace you have showered blessings on all. But by your sovereign grace you have showered on us the gifts of salvation, the indwelling presence of your Spirit, and all the spiritual gifts with which you have endowed us. How generous you have been with us.

So we now unite our voices and hearts to worship you this hour. We thank you for every good and perfect gift. Receive our worship in the name of the unspeakable gift, even Jesus Christ. Amen.

God Is Great

Call to Worship Texts

Deuteronomy 10:17
2 Samuel 7:22
1 Chronicles 16:25; 29:11
Psalm 48:1; 77:13; 95:1–3; 96:1–4; 104:1; 135:5;
　138:1–5; 145:1–3; 150:1–2
Isaiah 12:5–6
Jeremiah 10:6
Malachi 1:11

Responsive Call to Worship

Leader: Come, let us sing for joy to the Lord. Let us
　　　come before him with thanksgiving and extol
　　　him with music and song.

Men: For the Lord is the great God, the great King above all gods.

Women: In his hand are the depths of the earth and the mountain peaks belong to him. The sea is his, for he made it, and his hands formed the dry land.

Men: Great is the Lord and most worthy of praise, the great God, mighty and awesome.

Women: Praise him for his surpassing greatness which no one can fathom.

Unison: Yours, O Lord, is the greatness and the power and the glory and the majesty and the splendor, for everything in heaven and earth is yours. We extol you in the name of the Father, Son, and Holy Spirit. Amen.

Prayer of Adoration

How majestic is your name, O Lord God. We come to extol you through the exalted name of Jesus Christ. We bow in awe of your majesty. We marvel at your greatness in creating the wonders of this planet and the galaxies that surround us. We marvel at the greatness of your plan to choose, save, and preserve us through union with Jesus Christ. We marvel at your plan to bring us into your majestic eternal kingdom. How small our largest problems become as we see them in the light of your awesome presence.

We confess that our limited grasp of who you are can't begin to comprehend your character. Each day holds forth new opportunities to grow in our understanding of your greatness. Each day offers occasions to honor you. So we come this first day of a new week asking your help to honor you. Touch our minds and emotions and will as we worship you. Send us forth with hearts full of awe and overflowing with joy. Send us forth with firm trust because you are our majestically great and awesome Lord. Through Christ we pray. Amen.

God Is Holy

Call to Worship Texts

Exodus 15:11
Leviticus 19:2
1 Samuel 2:2
Psalm 29:2; 30:4; 47:8; 48:1; 93:5; 97:12; 99:5, 9;
   145:21
Isaiah 6:3
Ezekiel 39:7
Habakkuk 1:12–13
1 Peter 1:15–16
Revelation 4:8; 15:4

Responsive Call to Worship

Leader: Let us raise our voices to worship the Lord in the beauty of his holiness.

People: Holy, holy, holy is the Lord God Almighty, Father, Son, and Holy Spirit.

Leader: Let us now worship the Lord in the splendor of his holiness.

People: We have come to exalt the Lord our God and worship at his footstool.

89

Leader: We rejoice and praise his holy name through Christ, saying,

Unison: Holy, holy, holy is the Lord God Almighty, who was, and is, and is to come. Alleluia, Amen.

Prayer of Adoration

Holy Father, we now accept your invitation to draw near to you. We do so because of the work of Christ and in his holy name. We come to adore you for the beauty of your holiness. We confess that the sum of all moral excellence is found in you. Not the slightest moral blemish or sin has ever been found in your Son or Spirit. So we gather to express thanks at the remembrance of your holiness.

Holy One, we come with a sense of reverence knowing we are treading on holy ground. We come asking that you accept the imperfect praise which we lift to you this hour. Help us to go forth at the end of the hour to glorify you with holy lives and holy speech all during this new week. This we pray in the holy name of Christ the spotless Lamb, whom we adore, and who taught us to pray, saying, Our Father . . .

 God Is Jealous

Call to Worship Texts

Exodus 20:4–6; 34:14
Deuteronomy 4:24; 5:8–10; 6:15
Nahum 1:2

Responsive Call to Worship

Leader: Do not worship any other god, for the Lord, whose name is Jealous, is a jealous God.

Men: We will not make for ourselves an idol in the form of anything in heaven above or on the earth beneath or in the waters below.

Women: We will not bow down to them or worship them.

Men: For the Lord our God is a jealous God.

Women: He is a consuming fire, a jealous God.

Unison: So we come to worship and love the Lord our God with all our hearts and with all our souls and with all our minds. Praise belongs to the one and only Father, Son, and Holy Spirit, who deserve our undivided allegiance!

Prayer of Adoration

Our loving Lord, receive the adoration which we now offer you through our one and only Savior, Jesus Christ, the Way, the Truth, and the Life.

We come to acknowledge that you by nature are a jealous God. Your name is Jealous. We realize that this is not the ugly, selfish jealousy we see exhibited among humans. But you are properly jealous for the affections of those with whom you have entered into covenant. After creating and redeeming us, you have a right to receive our total loyalty and allegiance.

We acknowledge how it must grieve you when your people turn their backs and give affection and loyalty to idolatrous objects and beings. How patient you have been when your bride has wandered astray and committed spiritual adultery. You are rightly jealous because you love us and care so much for us as our Creator and Redeemer.

So we desire to give you all the praise and adoration you deserve with all our hearts, souls, and minds. We love you and desire to serve you. Receive our sincere worship as we raise our voices to pray through Christ the prayer he taught us, saying, Our Father . . .

God Is Just

Call to Worship Texts

Deuteronomy 32:4
2 Chronicles 19:7
Nehemiah 9:33
Job 37:23
Psalm 7:17; 9:8–9; 11:7; 67:4; 89:14; 97:1–2, 6; 98:8–9; 99:4; 129:4; 145:17
Jeremiah 9:24
1 John 1:9
Revelation 15:3–4

Responsive Call to Worship

Leader: Lift your voices to praise the Lord God because all his ways are just.

People: We give thanks to the Lord because of his righteousness and justice. We will sing praise to the name of the Lord Most High.

Leader: You have promised to judge the world in righteousness and govern the people with justice.

People: Righteousness and justice are the foundation
of your throne. As we confess our sins you are
faithful and just to forgive us our sins and
purify us from all unrighteousness. Therefore
we enter your presence this morning to honor
you, Father, Son, and Holy Spirit, because all
your ways are just.

Prayer of Adoration

Lord God Almighty, we bow in adoration because
you by nature are a just God. Everything you do is
ultimately fair and just. We praise you for the purity
of your justice. You conform fully to what is morally
and legally right because you are just. The psalmist
reminds us that righteousness and justice are the
foundation of your throne. Your justice upholds the
order of the universe and guarantees the safety of all
who put their trust in you.

Judge of all the earth, you know we live in a world
in which we often see an absence of justice. We
endure times of being treated unfairly. But we will
never have to face that in your treatment of us. You
will one day balance the present scales of injustice.
Thank you that you are faithful and just to forgive
us our sins. You treat us not only justly, but you go
beyond that and extend mercy, giving us what we
don't deserve. Therefore we set aside this hour to
praise and worship and adore you for the purity of
your justice. Please accept our homage which we
offer in the holy and just name of Jesus Christ.
Amen.

✝ God Is Light

Call to Worship Texts
Psalm 18:28; 27:1; 104:1–2
Isaiah 45:5–7
Habakkuk 3:4
Matthew 4:16
John 1:4–5; 8:12
1 Timothy 6:16
1 John 1:5
Revelation 22:5

Responsive Call to Worship

Leader: God said, Let there be light! And there was light.

People: The people walking in darkness have seen a great light.

Leader: On those living in the land of the shadow of death a light has dawned.

People: Christ came as the light of our world. Whoever follows him will never walk in darkness, but will have the light of life.

Leader: So we come into the light of his presence to worship him saying,

Unison: We praise you, O Father, Son, and Holy Spirit that you are light and in you is no darkness at all. Alleluia.

Prayer of Adoration

God of heaven, we call upon your name through Jesus Christ, the light of the world. Out of the void of darkness you spoke and light appeared on this planet.

Out of the darkness of sin you spoke through the prophets and predicted the coming of a great light. You fulfilled that promise as the light of the star guided the wise men to find the child who had been born, the one who later claimed to be the light of the world.

Father, we acknowledge that we have now entered into the light of the presence of Jesus Christ. We have come to worship you. Please manifest the light of your presence this hour. Please shine the light of your presence into our lives so we might leave this place glowing with the light of having been with you. This we pray in the name of Jesus Christ, the light of the world. Amen.

God Is Living (Source of Life)

Call to Worship Texts

Nehemiah 9:5–6
Psalm 18:46; 42:1–2; 84:1–2
Jeremiah 10:10
John 5:24–27; 10:10; 11:25–26; 14:6
Revelation 1:17–18

Responsive Call to Worship

Leader: In the beginning God created the heavens and the earth.

People: Then God said, Let us make man in our image, in our likeness.

Leader: So God created man in his own image, in the image of God he created him; male and female he created them.

95

People: And the Lord God formed man from the dust of the ground and breathed into his nostrils the breath of life.

Leader: And man became a living being.

People: When we consider your heavens, the work of your fingers, the moon and the stars, which you have set in place,

Leader: What is man that you are mindful of him, the son of man that you care for him?

Unison: You made him a little lower than the heavenly beings and crowned him with glory and honor. Therefore we raise our voices to honor you as the Creator of all human life. O living Lord, receive our praise this hour!

Prayer of Adoration

Our Father and living God, we now draw near to you knowing that you have drawn near to us. As Creator you have breathed into us the breath of life. Now we wish to use that breath to praise you.

You as the living God are the ultimate source of all life, the Creator of all living plants, animals, and humans. From the smallest, simplest forms of life to the most complex, we see evidence of your creative hands. Thank you for giving to us the gift of life, not only physical life, but especially for taking us who were spiritually dead and raising us to new life. We have crossed over from death to life. We can now live forever. You have filled us with newness of life which we desire to exhibit to a dying world. May the fullness of your life show in our lives, not only during this service, but throughout this new week.

O living God, Father, Son, and Spirit, how we long to enjoy fellowship with you. Fill us with adoration as we honor you in the name of your resurrected Son, Jesus Christ. Amen.

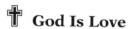 God Is Love

Call to Worship Texts

Psalm 103:8, 13, 17
Proverbs 15:9
Jeremiah 31:3
John 3:16; 14:21
Romans 5:8; 8:39
Ephesians 2:4–5
1 John 3:1
1 John 4:8–10, 16

Responsive Call to Worship

Leader: Praise the Lord, O my soul, and forget not all his benefits.

People: He has loved us with an everlasting love; he has crowned us with loving-kindness.

Leader: Because of his great love for us, God, who is rich in mercy, made us alive with Christ even when we were dead in transgressions.

People: God demonstrates his own love for us in this: While we were still sinners Christ died for us.

Leader: Neither the present nor the future, nor any powers, neither height nor depth, nor anything

97

else in all creation, will be able to separate us from the love of God that is in Christ Jesus our Lord.

Unison: Therefore we assemble this Sunday to rejoice and worship our Lord Jesus Christ for his loving nature and countless acts of love for us. Alleluia. Amen.

Prayer of Adoration

Lord God and beloved Father, we come into your presence with hearts overflowing with love. We recall your many demonstrations of unchanging love for us. Year after year you have acted in love toward us, even during those periods when we have failed to return your love as we should have. You have loved us with everlasting love from before the foundation of the world. You have chosen and adopted us in love not because of any act of faith or even any good which you foresaw in us, but purely out of love according to the good pleasure of your will. While we were still sinners you supremely demonstrated love for us in the sacrifice of your only beloved Son on Golgotha. We are challenged by Christ's love for needy and hurting people during his earthly ministry—reaching out to the lonely and the hungry and the frightened and the guilty.

We now come asking for your help to grow in our love for you this year. Help us during this hour to express adoration in ways that will stir us to love you in all we do during the week. Help us to reflect your love toward others. This we pray because we love the One who taught us to pray, saying, Our Father . . .

✝ God Is Merciful

Call to Worship Texts

Exodus 34:6–7
1 Chronicles 16:34
2 Chronicles 5:13
Nehemiah 9:17
Psalm 57:9–11; 103:2–4, 11; 116:5; 145:8–10
2 Corinthians 1:2–3
Ephesians 2:4–5
Hebrews 4:16
1 Peter 1:3

Responsive Call to Worship

Leader: Let us approach the throne of grace with confidence, so that we may receive mercy.

People: We approach the Lord, the compassionate and gracious God, slow to anger, abounding in love and faithfulness, maintaining love to thousands, and forgiving wickedness, rebellion, and sin.

Leader: God, who is rich in mercy, made us alive with Christ even when we were dead in trespasses.

People: In his great mercy he has given us new birth into a living hope.

Leader: So as a church family we worship him saying,

Unison: Praise be to the God and Father of our Lord Jesus Christ! He has demonstrated the riches of his mercy to us. Praise be to the merciful God and Father of our Lord Jesus Christ!

Prayer of Adoration

Our Father of mercies, we give thanks to you for your mercy which endures forever. We come, both married and single, both men and women, both young and old, and unite our voices to praise you for the mercy you have shown to us.

We acknowledge your general mercies which you have given to all people—the temporal blessings of health, food, homes, families, and the ability to laugh. Even those who ignore you have benefited from your general mercies.

But most of all we thank you for your sovereign mercies given to your special people through Christ. You have taken the initiative to forgive us our sins time and again. How merciful you have been to us when we deserved punishment. Our hearts are stirred with deep gratitude. As high as the heavens are above the earth, so great is your mercy toward each of us in this room who fear you. So we've entered into your special presence to praise you. Please accept our worship and fill us with new devotion to you. This we ask in the name of Jesus Christ the Master. Amen.

✝ God Is Omnipotent

Call to Worship Texts

Deuteronomy 3:24
Joshua 4:24
1 Chronicles 29:11–12
2 Chronicles 20:6
Job 9:4–9; 26:12, 14

Psalm 21:13; 29:1–4; 62:11; 66:3, 7; 77:14; 93:1;
147:5
Jeremiah 10:6, 12–13; 27:5
Nahum 1:3–4
Romans 1:20
Ephesians 1:19–21
Revelation 4:11; 11:16–17; 19:1, 6

Responsive Call to Worship

Leader: Let us, the people of Christ's church, lift our
voices this hour to magnify the unlimited power
of God the Father, Son, and Holy Spirit.

Congregation: We acknowledge your incomparably
great power at work in us who believe. That
power is the same divine energy which was
demonstrated in Christ when you raised him
from the dead and gave him the place of highest
honor in heaven—a place that is infinitely supe-
rior to any command, authority, power, or control. We praise you for the strength of the Spirit's
inner reinforcement.

Leader: Therefore we lift our voices to now sing:

Sing in unison: All hail the power of Jesus' name! Let
angels prostrate fall. Bring forth the royal diadem, And crown him Lord of all; Bring forth the
royal diadem, And crown him Lord of all! Amen.

Prayer of Adoration

Lord God Almighty, Lord Sabaoth, it's with a sense
of wonder that we approach your throne. We come
before your face only through the name and merits

of Jesus Christ. We come desiring to sense your presence and experience your power.

We praise the fullness of your universal power. All that you are is saturated with eternal energy and forceful effectiveness. Nothing is too hard for you. You are supreme in your authority and absolute in your ability.

Please fill us anew with the power of your indwelling Holy Spirit. Help us magnify your name this hour as we worship through Christ whose power is at work in us to do above and beyond all that we ask or think. This we pray in his mighty name. Amen.

God Is Omnipresent

Call to Worship Texts

Psalm 95:1–2; 100:1–2; 140:13
Isaiah 66:1
Jeremiah 23:23–24
Matthew 18:20; 28:20
1 Corinthians 16:22–23

Responsive Call to Worship

Leader: Come, O Lord!

Men: Let us sing with joy to our Lord.

Women: Let us come before his presence with joyful songs.

Men: Because the Lord of heaven and earth does not live in temples built by hands.

Women: Heaven is his throne and the earth is his footstool.

Men: His presence fills heaven and earth. No one can hide in secret places so that the Lord cannot see him.

Women: Yet the omnipresent God has promised us that where two or three come together in the name of Christ he is among us.

Unison: Praise be to Christ, who is with us in this assembly, and who has promised to remain with us always to the very end of the age.

Prayer of Adoration

As a deer pants for streams of water, so our souls pant for you, O Lord God. We have looked forward to entering your presence with thanksgiving. What a privilege to come before you through Jesus Christ, who is among us in this church this very hour. Grant us a growing awareness of your presence throughout this service.

We know that the whole universe is alive with your personal presence. You are not confined to any one geographical location. As transcendent Creator you are also imminent in all places. You have promised never to leave us. You have promised to come among us in a special way when we assemble like this on the first day of the week. In your presence we experience fullness of joy. So please help us to set aside distracting thoughts. Defeat any hindrances of the archenemy. Fill us freshly by the power of your indwelling Spirit that we might magnify you—in the name of Christ we pray. Amen.

God Is Omniscient

Call to Worship Texts

1 Samuel 2:3
1 Kings 8:39
Job 21:22; 36:4
Psalm 1:6; 44:21; 139:1–6; 147:4–5
Isaiah 46:9–10
Luke 16:15
Romans 11:33–36
2 Timothy 2:19
Hebrews 4:13

Responsive Call to Worship

Leader: Nothing in all creation is hidden from God's sight. Everything is uncovered and laid bare before the eyes of him to whom we must give account.

Men: The Lord is a God who knows, and by him deeds are weighed.

Women: He knows the secrets of the heart.

Men: And yet he still accepts us by his grace.

Women: The Lord knows those who are his; he knows the way of the righteous.

Men: He knows the end from the beginning.

Women: He determines the number of the stars and calls them each by its name.

Leader: His understanding has no limit.

Unison: Therefore we lift our voices in adoration proclaiming, O the depth of the riches of the wisdom and knowledge of God! How unsearchable his judgments, and his paths beyond tracing out! To him be the glory forever! Amen.

Prayer of Adoration

Lord God, we bow before you to express our adoration. You are the God of unlimited knowledge, knowledge of the past, present, and future. You know everything about us. You know when we sit and when we rise. You perceive our thoughts in advance. Before a word is on our tongue, you know it completely. Such knowledge is too wonderful for us. How we praise you.

This Lord's Day we marvel that your knowledge extends to every scientific theory, every technological advance, every medical discovery. Knowledge as yet uncovered by the most brilliant of humans is already in your possession and has always been. Even the secrets we have hidden are open to your gaze. How we marvel at your omniscience.

Help us this day to give you that honor you deserve, to worship you in spirit and in truth. May we be sent forth to praise you wherever we go in the days of this new week. We turn our attention away from ourselves and toward you. We rejoice in your presence and lift our praise in the name of Jesus Christ. Amen.

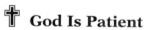 God Is Patient

Call to Worship Texts
Exodus 34:6
Numbers 14:18

Nehemiah 9:17
Psalm 86:15; 103:8–10
Joel 2:13
Nahum 1:3

Responsive Call to Worship

Leader: Let us join in praising the triune God who by nature is patient.

People: The Lord is compassionate and gracious, slow to anger, abounding in love and faithfulness.

Leader: He will not always accuse, nor will he harbor his anger forever.

People: He does not treat us as our sins deserve or repay us according to our iniquities.

Leader: As a father has compassion on his children, so the Lord has compassion on those who fear him. For he knows how we are formed, he remembers that we are dust.

Unison: May the God who gives endurance and encouragement give us a spirit of unity as we follow Christ Jesus, so that with one heart and mouth we may glorify the God and Father of our Lord Jesus Christ. We thank him for his patience in dealing with us! May he be exalted!

Prayer of Adoration

Father, we enter your presence this Sunday to honor you in the name of your Son and in the power of your Spirit. We thank you for the patience which graces your perfect character. We address you as the God of patience. You have demonstrated patience countless times down through history in your dealings with your people. From earliest times in the days of Noah, Abraham, Moses, Jonah, and David you have exercised your powers of self-restraint. You were patient in dealing with the wayward and rebellious children of Israel. You were willing to bear and forbear with them. You were slow to anger, slow to punish.

Father, we acknowledge that you have also been patient in dealing with us. How patient and merciful and loving you have been when we were slow to learn and sometimes stubborn. We ask your forgiveness for the sins which we have repeatedly committed against you and others. We have not always been patient in times of testing. We have even complained against you on occasion and withdrawn from the race. Forgive us through Christ. Thank you for the patience of your Spirit in transforming us into the image of Christ. Help us to reflect the Spirit's fruit of patience this week as we grow in grace and the knowledge of Christ. We pray this in his name and with the words he taught us, saying, Our Father . . .

 ## God Is Sovereign

Call to Worship Texts

Exodus 15:18
Deuteronomy 4:39
Joshua 2:11
1 Samuel 2:6–8
2 Kings 19:15
1 Chronicles 29:11–12

2 Chronicles 20:6
Nehemiah 9:5–6
Job 12:9–10
Psalm 22:28–29; 24:1; 47:2–3, 7–8; 66:7; 74:12; 83:18; 89:11; 93:1–2; 115:3; 135:5–6
Isaiah 40:21–23
Jeremiah 10:10; 18:6
Lamentations 5:19
Ezekiel 17:24
Acts 17:24
Romans 14:11
Ephesians 4:6
1 Timothy 6:15–16
Revelation 4:11; 19:6

Responsive Call to Worship

Leader: Come, let us bow down and worship the One seated on the throne above, the One whom we own as our sovereign King and Lord.

Unison: You alone are the Lord. You made the heavens, even the highest heavens, and all their starry host, the earth and all that is on it, the seas and all that is in them. You give life to everything. Yours, O Lord, is the kingdom; you are exalted as head over all. Wealth and honor come from you; you are the ruler of all things. In your hands are strength and power to exalt and give strength to all. Now, our God, we in this church set aside this hour to give you thanks and to praise your glorious name as our sovereign Lord and King. To you we lift our homage. Amen.

Prayer of Adoration

Lord God, our Sovereign King, we who are subjects of your kingdom bow before your exalted throne. We gather to lift our prayers and praise in the name of our Lord Jesus Christ and with the aid of your indwelling Spirit.

Today we focus on your sovereignty. You are now exalted on your throne, above all creatures in heaven and on earth. You rule over all nations. No king, president, or dictator occupies an equal position with you. You are supreme, even over Satan and his forces of darkness. Thus we acknowledge that you have the right to do only and always what pleases you. The counsel of your will is always good and wise. In all things you are able to work for the good of those who love you.

We thank you for the way your sovereign hand worked in the lives of Abraham, Joseph, Moses, Daniel, Peter, and Paul. But we also thank you that you continue to work sovereignly in our lives today, sustaining us through our most difficult times of testing. Help us to recognize and submit to your supremacy over us.

We ask that you might now receive the adoration that comes from our hearts. We bow before your throne to acknowledge you as the reigning sovereign. We exalt you through Jesus Christ whom we own as Lord of lords and King of kings. Amen.

God Is Truthful

Call to Worship Texts

Numbers 23:19
Deuteronomy 32:4

> 1 Samuel 15:29
> Psalm 25:10; 31:5; 117
> Jeremiah 10:10
> John 14:6; 17:17

Responsive Call to Worship

Leader: We assemble to worship the triune God who is the source of all truth.

Congregation: We acknowledge that our God is not a human that he should ever lie or change his mind. When he speaks he acts. When he promises he brings it to fulfillment. He is the God of truth whose truth endures forever. We honor you, O Lord, through our Lord Jesus Christ, who is the way, the truth, and the life. Amen.

Prayer of Adoration

Our Father in heaven, accept our worship this hour which we desire to present in spirit and in truth through Christ. We render worship because you by nature are a truthful God. Your character is marked by unblemished integrity. You aren't human that you should ever lie. Not only is truth inherent in your being, but truth is evident in your Word as well. We can trust your character and trust your Word. We can trust the veracity of every word which you have ever spoken. All of your promises and all of your commands are totally true. How we praise you that your truth will endure from generation to generation. Help us to reflect your truth in all of our words and deeds throughout this new week. This we pray, worshiping you through the name of Jesus Christ who is the way, the truth, and the life. Amen.

God Is Unchanging

Call to Worship Texts

Numbers 23:19
Deuteronomy 32:3–4
1 Samuel 15:29
2 Samuel 22:47
Psalm 33:11; 102:25–27
Isaiah 40:7–8
Malachi 3:6
Hebrews 13:8
James 1:17

Responsive Call to Worship

Leader: We lift our voices to praise the One who said, I the Lord do not change.

People: He who is the Glory of Israel does not lie or change his mind; for he is not a human, that he should change his mind.

Leader: The plans of the Lord stand firm forever, the purposes of his heart through all generations.

People: Even the heavens and the earth will perish, but the Lord remains. They will all wear out like a garment. But he remains the same.

Leader: He is the Father of the heavenly lights, who does not change like shifting shadows.

Unison: Praise be to the Lord our Rock! Exalted be God the Rock through Jesus Christ, who is the same yesterday and today and forever. Amen.

Prayer of Adoration

We rejoice, Lord God our Rock, at the thought of your unchanging nature. We can totally trust and rely on you without any fear that you will be inconsistent or fickle in dealing with us. We can depend on you to keep your word and to continue to show the same traits of character which you have revealed in Scripture and which you have demonstrated in dealings with your people down through history.

We come before your throne through Christ, the one who is the Alpha and Omega, who always has existed without finite beginning and who always will exist.

Father, we are bombarded in our daily lives with change on every hand—changes that are exciting and beneficial for humans and other changes that are to our detriment. We struggle to keep up with the knowledge explosion in the workplace and are concerned about our job security—if we are fortunate enough to have a job. We see changes in people who we once thought were our friends, and whom we no longer can trust. So today in the midst of the whirling changes which surround us we especially appreciate the stability and reliability we have come to experience in your unchanging character as our Rock.

Open our eyes and ears this hour as we look into your Word. May you, the One who changes not, use your Word to change us in ways that will result in your glory. Use your Word in this service to infuse us with new hope in your ability to change our lives and the lives of those around us. May Jesus Christ be exalted in this assembly. We worship and now pray through the name of the One who is the same yesterday, today, and forever. Amen.

God Is Unified

Call to Worship Texts

Deuteronomy 6:4–5
1 Kings 8:60
Isaiah 44:6; 45:5
Mark 12:29–30
1 Corinthians 8:6
Galatians 3:20
1 Timothy 2:5

Responsive Call to Worship

Leader: God is one! Let us unite our voices to praise the Father, Son, and Holy Spirit for existing in perfect unity and harmony.

Congregation: For us there is but one God, the Father, from whom all things come and for whom we live; there is but one Lord, Jesus Christ, through whom all things came and through whom we live. May all the peoples of the earth know that the Lord is our God and there is no other. We unite our hearts as we proclaim that we love the Lord our God with all our heart and with all our soul and with all our strength. Blessed be the Father, Son, and Holy Spirit who continue to live in perfect harmony, today and forevermore.

Prayer of Adoration

Lord God, we assemble to unite our voices in your presence. In spite of outward differences in appearance and inward differences in tastes and interests and backgrounds, we agree on your worthiness to be honored as our one and only true God. We believe that you exist in three persons yet as one being in perfect harmony. The mystery of the tri-unity is beyond our human categories to exhaust. So we bow in hushed silence, conscious of your transcendence.

We worship you for the perfect harmony which has existed in your being from eternity. Friction does not spoil the unity inherent in your being. Mutual love between you and your Son and Spirit challenges us to display unity in the church which bears your name.

We now unite in worship, conscious of our unity with all true believers in all places and times, in heaven and earth, many of whom are gathering in worship on this day. As members of the one, holy, universal and apostolic church, we lift our voices in praise. Along with the hosts of heaven above we render adoration through Jesus Christ, who now lives and reigns with you, and the Holy Spirit, one God, who is now in our midst. Amen.

God Is Wise

Call to Worship Texts
Job 12:13
Psalm 104:24
Proverbs 3:19–20; 9:10

Isaiah 28:29; 40:28
Jeremiah 10:12
Daniel 2:20–21
Romans 11:33–34
Ephesians 3:10–11
Colossians 2:3
Revelation 5:11–12; 7:12

Responsive Call to Worship

Leader: Praise be to the name of God forever and ever. All wisdom is his. Let us now worship him through Jesus Christ in whom are hidden all the treasures of wisdom and knowledge.

Congregation: The Lord gives wisdom to the wise and knowledge to the discerning. He reveals deep and hidden things. He knows what lies in darkness. Oh, the depth of the riches of the wisdom and knowledge of God! Who has been his counselor? His intent was that now, through the church, the manifold wisdom of God should be made known to the rulers and authorities in the heavenly realms. May the Lord's manifold wisdom be known through this church as we worship him this day!

Prayer of Adoration

We bow to acknowledge, O Father, that the reverent fear of you is the beginning of wisdom. So we come with humble reverence. We come from a busy week to set aside time to honor you through Christ. We praise you for the unlimited wisdom that pervades your being—the wisdom which you have made available to us as well. How we need your wisdom in facing the decisions, challenges, and tests of daily life.

We come marveling at your magnificent wisdom evident in the universe which surrounds us. How wisely you created plant and animal life. How wisely you ordained the laws of physics and chemistry. How wisely you suspended the planets and stars in space. How wisely you made us in your image. The more we study your works of nature, the more we stand amazed.

But we especially thank you for the wisdom displayed in your plan to redeem us sinners through Jesus Christ. You have chosen the weak and foolish things of the world to confound the wise. Your intent was that through the church your manifold wisdom should be made known to rulers and authorities in the heavenly realms. Help us to reflect your wisdom. Accept the sincere praise we now lift to you through Christ in whom are hidden all the treasures of wisdom and knowledge. Amen.

PART 2

Service Models

8

Communion Services

Baptist

✝ Communion Hymn

✝ Invitation to the Table

Let all who have repented of their sins, who have accepted Jesus Christ as their personal Savior and Lord, and who are in fellowship with his church, receive with thanksgiving the bread and cup, in remembrance of our crucified and resurrected Lord.

✝ Prayer of Confession

✝ Words of Institution

Read 1 Corinthians 11:23–29 or Matthew 26:20–30.

✝ Prayer of Thanks for the Broken Body of Christ

✝ Distribution and Partaking of Bread

"He took bread, gave thanks and broke it, and gave it to them, saying, 'This is my body given for you; do this in remembrance of me'" (Luke 22:19).

✝ Prayer of Thanks for the Shed Blood of Christ

✝ Distribution and Partaking of Cup

"After taking the cup, he gave thanks and said, 'Take this and divide it among you. For I tell you I will not drink again of the fruit of the vine until the kingdom of God comes'" (Luke 22:17–18).

✝ Closing Hymn and Benediction

"May the God of peace, who through the blood of the eternal covenant brought back from the dead our Lord Jesus, that great Shepherd of the sheep, equip you with everything good for doing his will, and may he work in us what is pleasing to him, through Jesus Christ, to whom be glory for ever and ever. Amen" (Hebrews 13:20–21).

Christian Reformed Church

Following the Service of the Word.

Minister: Brothers and sisters in Christ, the Gospels tell us that on the first day of the week, the day on which our Lord rose from the dead, he appeared to some of his disciples and was made known to them in the breaking of bread. Come, then, to the joyful feast of our Lord.

If the communion elements are not already on the table, they may be brought forward at this point.

✝ The Thanksgiving

Minister: Lift up your hearts.

People: We lift them up to the Lord.

Minister: Let us give thanks to the Lord our God.

People: It is right for us to give thanks. It is our joy and our peace, at all times and in all places, to give thanks to you, holy Father, almighty, everlasting God, through Christ our Lord.

Minister: We bless you for your continual love and care for every creature. We praise you for forming us in your image and calling us to be your people. We thank you that you did not abandon us in our rebellion against your love, but sent prophets and teachers to lead us into the way of salvation. Above all we thank you for sending Jesus your Son to deliver us from the way of sin and death by the obedience of his life, by his suffering upon the cross, and by his resurrection from the dead. We praise you that he now reigns with you in glory and ever lives to pray for us. We thank you for the Holy Spirit, who leads us into truth, defends us in adversity, and out of every people unites us into one holy church. Therefore with the whole company of saints in heaven and on earth we worship and glorify you, God most holy, and we sing with joy.

All sing:

Holy! Holy! Holy! Lord God Almighty!
All thy works shall praise thy Name,
   in earth and sky and sea.
Holy, Holy, Holy, Merciful and Mighty!
God in Three Persons, blessed Trinity!

✝ The Institution

We give thanks to God the Father that our Savior, Jesus Christ, before he suffered, gave us this memorial of this sacrifice, until his coming again. For the Lord Jesus on the night when he was betrayed took bread, and when he had given thanks, he broke it, and said, "This is my body which is for you. Do this in remembrance of me." In the same way also the cup, after supper, saying, "This cup is the new covenant in my blood. Do this, as often as you drink it, in remembrance of me." For as often as you eat this bread and drink the cup, you proclaim the Lord's death until he comes.

✝ The Memorial

All: We shall do as our Lord commands.
We proclaim that our Lord was sent by the Father
into the world, that he took upon himself our
flesh and blood,
and bore the wrath of God against our sin.
We confess that he was condemned to die
that we might be pardoned
and suffered death that we might live.
We proclaim that he is risen
to make us right with God,
and that he shall come again
in the glory of his new creation.
This we do now
and until he comes again.

✝ Prayer of Consecration

Minister: Heavenly Father, show forth among us the
presence of your life-giving Word and Holy Spirit,
to sanctify us and your whole church through
this sacrament. Grant that all who share the body
and blood of our Savior Jesus Christ may be one
in him, and remain faithful in love and hope.

And as this grain has been gathered from many
fields into one loaf, and these grapes from many
hills into one cup, grant, O Lord, that your whole

church may soon be gathered from the ends of the earth into your kingdom.

Now as our Savior Christ has taught us to pray:

All: Our Father who art in heaven . . .

☩ Preparation of the Elements

(As the minister breaks the bread and pours the cup)

Minister: The bread which we break is a sharing in the body of Christ.

People: We who are many are one body, for we all share the same loaf.

Minister: The cup for which we give thanks is a sharing in the blood of Christ.

People: The cup which we drink is our participation in the blood of Christ.

☩ The Invitation

Congregation in the Lord Jesus Christ, the Lord has prepared his table for all who love him and trust in him alone for their salvation. All who are truly sorry for their sins, who sincerely believe in the Lord Jesus as their Savior, and who desire to live in obedience to him, are now invited to come with gladness to the table of the Lord.

☩ The Dedication

All: Holy Father, in thanks for the sacrifice of Jesus Christ, in the joy of his resurrection, in the hope of his coming again, we present ourselves a living sacrifice and come to the table of our Lord.

(As the minister indicates the elements)
Minister: The gifts of God for the people of God.

✝ The Communion

(When the people are ready to eat the bread)
Minister: Take, eat, remember and believe that the body of our Lord Jesus Christ was given for a complete remission of all our sins.

(When the people are ready to drink the cup)
Minister: Take, drink, remember and believe that the precious blood of our Lord Jesus Christ was shed for a complete remission of all our sins.

✝ The Thanksgiving

Minister: Congregation in Christ, since the Lord has fed us at his table, let us praise his holy name with thanksgiving.
All: Bless the Lord, O my soul; and all that is within me, bless his holy name. Bless the Lord, O my soul, and forget not all his benefits. Who forgives all your iniquity, who heals all your diseases. Who redeems your life from destruction, who crowns you with steadfast love and mercy. Who satisfies you with good as long as you live *(Psalm 103)*.
All: *(Hymn—optional)*

✝ The Dismissal

Minister: The peace of God which passes all understanding keep your hearts and minds in the

knowledge and love of God, and of his Son
Jesus Christ, our Lord: and the blessing of God
almighty, Father, Son, and Holy Spirit, be
among you and remain with you always.

People: Amen.

Minister: Go in peace to love and serve the Lord.

All: (Hymn—optional)

Methodist

✝ The Invitation

You who truly and earnestly repent of your sins, who live in love and peace with your neighbors, and who intend to lead a new life, following the commandments of God and walking henceforth in His holy ways, draw near with faith, and take this holy sacrament for your comfort; and humbly bowing make your honest confession to Almighty God.

✝ The General Confession

Almighty God, our Heavenly Father, Maker of all things, Judge of all people, who with great mercy has promised forgiveness and deliverance to all who turn to You with hearty repentance and true faith, we confess that we have sinned against You and are hopeless without Your grace. Have mercy upon us, O merciful Father, have mercy upon us; pardon and deliver us from all our sins:

from blindness of heart and lack of love,
from the deceits of the world, the flesh, and the devil,
from false doctrine and neglect of Your Word,
from anxiety and lack of trust.

127

O God, our Savior, keep us this day without sin. Give us strength to serve and please You in newness of life, and to honor and praise Your name, through Jesus Christ our Lord. Amen.

✝ The Petition

Almighty God, You have so faithfully watched over us, and so graciously helped us; now hear our petitions:

for good health and sound minds,

for strength to earn our bread, for rest from worry and labor,

for safety in travel, for protection from enemies,

for Christian homes, for a just and strong nation.

Out of Your compassion give us those things which are good and proper for our souls, and protect us by Your might in all our tribulations. Grant us in this world the peace that is from above, and bring us to everlasting life in the world to come, through Christ our Lord, who taught us to pray saying:

Our Father, which art in heaven . . .

✝ The Intercession

Almighty God, who created the world from nothing, and who sustains it by Your powerful word, support and protect us that we may serve You as intercessors in Your world; and to that end hear our prayers for those in need: for the sick, the infirm and the dying; for widows and orphans, the poor and oppressed; for the lonely, discouraged, bereaved and heartbroken; for those in bondage to sin, unmindful of God, without knowledge of the gospel of salvation.

We pray too for all Your servants who work honorably in the cause of our Lord Jesus Christ:

for homemakers and wage earners,

for teachers and students,

for doctors and nurses and others who serve the
   sick,

for laborers and executives,

for farmers and city dwellers,

for the aged and the young,

for those who govern and those who are ruled,

to each of these and to all others for whom we should pray, give wisdom, strength, and the power to endure, through Jesus Christ our Lord. Amen.

✝ Communion Hymn

✝ The Dialogue

Minister: The Lord be with you.

People: And also with you.

Minister: Lift up your hearts.

People: We lift them up to the Lord.

Minister: Let us give thanks to the Lord.

People: It is right to give Him thanks and praise.

✝ Thanksgiving

We give You thanks, O Lord God, for all Your goodness at all times and in all places. You have shielded, rescued, helped, and guided us all our days and brought us to this hour, letting us once again worship You and seek Your help.

Blessed are You, Lord God, Ruler of all creation; for by Your goodness we have this bread from the soil and this fruit from the vine.

✝ Praise

Minister: It is always right and proper that we should give You thanks and praise, O Lord God, for You alone reign. You judge the world in righteousness and rule over all the nations. Therefore, with angels and archangels, and with all the inhabitants of heaven we honor and adore Your glorious name, evermore praising You and saying:

People: Holy, holy, holy, Lord God of hosts!
Heaven and earth are full of Your glory,
Glory be to You, O Lord most high. Amen.

✝ The Great Thanksgiving

Minister: Almighty God, You created us to enjoy Your fellowship, and even when we transgressed Your command, You did not forsake us, but chastened us as a merciful Father.

You called Abraham from the land of his fathers, and freed the children of Israel from bondage and slavery; You gave Your law and sent Your prophets to guide them in Your ways.

At the right time You gave the world Your only Son, who by His apostles and the church, called us to salvation. You adopted us and daily give us aid in the journey of faith by the same Spirit. Our hearts are full, O God, and in thanksgiving to You we cry, Abba, Father.

In confidence that You will bring us to our full inheritance and give us our place at the heavenly table with Your Son, our Savior, Jesus Christ, we offer thanksgiving, joining our voices with all the church to confess:

People: Christ has died,
Christ has risen,
Christ will come again.

✝ Glory to God

People: Glory be to the Father and to the Son and to the Holy Ghost; as it was in the beginning, is now, and ever shall be, world without end. Amen. Amen.

✝ Prayer of Approach

Almighty God, our heavenly Father, send the power of Your Holy Spirit upon us, that we may experience anew the suffering, death and resurrection of Your Son, Jesus Christ. May Your Spirit help us to know, in the breaking of this bread and the drinking of this cup, the presence of Christ who gave His body and blood for all. And may Your Spirit make us one with Christ, one with each other, and one in service to all the world. Amen.

✝ Words of Consecration

Minister, laying his hand upon the bread:

In the night of His betrayal, Jesus took bread, and when He had given thanks, He broke it and gave it to His disciples, saying, "Take, eat, this is My body which is given for you; do this in remembrance of me."

Minister, laying his hand upon the cup:

In like manner, after supper He took the cup, and when He had given thanks, He gave it to them, saying, "Drink of this, all of you, for this is My blood of the New Testament which is shed for you and for many, for the remission of sins; do this as often as you drink it, in remembrance of me."

✝ Words of Distribution

The body of our Lord Jesus Christ, which was given for you, preserve your soul and body unto everlasting life. Take and eat this in remembrance that Christ died for you, and feed upon Him in your heart, by faith with thanksgiving.

The blood of our Lord Jesus Christ, which was shed for you, preserve your soul and body unto everlasting life. Drink this in remembrance that Christ's blood was shed for you, and be thankful.

✝ Benediction

From *Pastor's Handbook,* Clyde E. Van Valin, editor (Indianapolis: Light and Life Press, 1991), pp. 127–31.

Zwinglian (Easter 1525, Zurich)

Prayer

The overseer or pastor turns toward the people and prays the following prayer with a loud, clear voice:

O Almighty, Eternal God, whom all creatures rightly honor, worship and praise as their Lord, Creator and Father: grant us poor sinners that with real constancy and faith we may perform Thy praise and thanksgiving, which Thine only begotten Son, our Lord and Savior Jesus Christ, hath commanded the faithful to do in memory of His death; through the same Jesus Christ, Thy Son, our Lord, who liveth and reigneth with Thee in unity with the Holy Spirit, God for ever and ever. Amen.

Scripture Reading

The server or lector says the following in a loud voice:

The Lection is found in the first Epistle of Paul to the Corinthians, the eleventh chapter (vv. 20–29).

Here the servers say with the whole church:

Praise be to God.

Hymn

Now the pastor begins the first verse of the following hymn of praise, and then the people—men and women—say the verses alternately, one after another.

Pastor: Glory be to God on high!

Men: And peace on earth!

Women: To men, a right will!

Men: We praise Thee, we bless Thee.

Women: We worship Thee, we glorify Thee.

Men: We give thanks to Thee for Thy great glory and goodness, O Lord God, heavenly King, Father Almighty!

Women: O Lord, Thou only-begotten Son, Jesus Christ, and the Holy Ghost.

Men: O Lord God, Thou Lamb of God, Son of the Father, Thou that takest away the sins of the world, have mercy upon us!

Women: Thou that takest away the sin of the world, receive our prayer!

Men: Thou that sittest at the right hand of the Father, have mercy upon us.

Women: For Thou only art holy.

Men: Thou only art the Lord.

Women: Thou only, O Jesus Christ, with the Holy Ghost, art most high in the glory of God the Father.

Men and Women: Amen.

Deacon or lector: The Lord be with you.

People: And with thy spirit.

✝ Gospel Reading

Lector: The following Lection from the Gospel is found in John, the sixth chapter.

People: Praise be to God.

Lector reads verses 47–63

Then the lector kisses the book and says:

Praise and thanks be to God. He willeth to forgive all our sins according to His holy Word.

People: Amen!

✝ Apostles' Creed

Server: I believe in one God,

Men: In the Father Almighty,

Women: And in Jesus Christ, His only-begotten Son, our Lord.

Men: Who was conceived by the Holy Ghost.

Women: Born of the Virgin Mary.

Men: Suffered under Pontius Pilate, was crucified, dead and buried.

Women: He descended into hell.

Men: The third day He rose again from the dead.

Women: He ascended into heaven.

Men: And sitteth on the right hand of God the Father Almighty.

Women: From thence He shall come to judge the quick and the dead.

Men: I believe in the Holy Ghost.

Women: The holy, universal Christian Church, the Communion of Saints.

Men: The forgiveness of sins.

Women: The resurrection of the body.

Men: And the life everlasting.

Men and Women: Amen.

✝ Instruction and Prayer

Dear brothers, in keeping with the observance and institution of our Lord Jesus Christ, we now desire to eat the bread and drink the cup which He has commanded us to use in commemoration, praise and thanksgiving that He suffered death for us and shed His blood to wash away our sin. Wherefore, let everyone call to mind, according to Paul's word, how much comfort, faith and assurance he has in the same Jesus Christ our Lord, lest anyone pretend to be a believer who is not, and so be guilty of the Lord's death. Neither let anyone commit offense against the whole Christian communion, which is the body of Christ.

Kneel, therefore, and pray:

Our Father, which art in heaven, hallowed be Thy name. Thy kingdom come. Thy will be done, in earth as it is in heaven. Give us our daily bread. Forgive us our debts, as we forgive our debtors. And lead us not into temptation, but deliver us from evil.

People: Amen.

Server: O Lord, God Almighty, who by Thy Spirit hast brought us together into Thy one body, in the unity of faith, and hast commanded that body to give Thee praise and thanks for Thy goodness and free gift in delivering Thine only-begotten Son, our Lord Jesus Christ, to death for our sins: grant that we may do the same so faithfully that we may not, by any pretense or deceit, provoke Thee who art the truth which cannot be deceived.

Grant also that we may live as purely as becometh Thy body, Thy family and Thy children, so that even the unbelieving may learn to recognize Thy name and glory. Keep us, Lord, that Thy name and glory may never be reviled because of our lives. O Lord, ever increase our faith, which is trust in Thee, Thou who livest and reignest, God for ever and ever. Amen.

✝ The Way Christ Instituted This Supper

Pastor reads 1 Corinthians 11:23–26. Then the designated servers carry around the unleavened bread, from which each one of the faithful takes a morsel or mouthful with his own hand, or has it offered to him by the server who carries the bread around. And when those with the bread have proceeded so far that everyone has eaten his small piece, the other servers then follow with the cup, and in the same manner give it to each person to drink. And all of this takes place with such honor and propriety as well becomes the Church of God and the Supper of Christ.

Afterwards the people having eaten and drunk, thanks is given to the example of Christ, by the use of Psalm 12, and the shepherd or pastor begins:

Pastor: Praise, O ye servants of the Lord, Praise the name of the Lord.

Men: Blessed be the name of the Lord, from this time forth and for evermore.

Women: From the rising of the sun unto the going down of the same the Lord's name is highly praised.

Men: The Lord is exalted above all nations and His glory above the heavens.

Women: Who is like unto the Lord our God, who sitteth so high and bendeth down to have care for the things in heaven and earth?

Men: He raiseth up the humble out of the dust and lifteth the poor out of the filth.

Women: That He may set him with princes, with the princes of His people.

Men: He maketh the barren woman of the house to be a mother, who has the joy of children.

Pastor: We give Thee thanks, O Lord, for all Thy gifts and blessings: Thou who livest and reignest, God for ever and ever.

People: Amen.

Pastor: Depart in peace.

From *Liturgies of the Western Church* (New York: William Collins, 1961), pp. 151–55.

Silent Communion Service
(Christmas Eve or Holy Week)

Printed program includes the following:

We gather this evening in obedience to the command of Christ to observe this meal until he returns. On the same night on which he was betrayed Jesus instituted this sacrament for the nourishment of his church. Through the years Christians have continued to meet in services like this to remember the broken body and shed blood of Christ.

Tonight this will be a silent service. Not a word will be spoken. Please enter with a readiness to worship. You are encouraged to meditate on Christ's birth, life, atoning death, resurrection on the third day, ascension to the right hand of the Father, and promised second coming.

 Prelude and Lighting of Candles

 Processional

Congregation stands as minister and elders/deacons come forward.

 Moments of Meditation

Solo: O Little Town of Bethlehem or O Sacred Head Now Wounded (Option: print story of writing of hymn in program).

✟ Silent Prayer

Almighty Father, whose dear Son, on the night before he suffered, instituted the Sacrament of his Body and Blood: Mercifully grant that we may receive it thankfully in remembrance of Jesus Christ our Lord, who in these holy mysteries gives us a pledge of eternal life; and who now lives and reigns with you and the Holy Spirit, one God, for ever and ever. Amen *(Book of Common Prayer).*

✟ Invitation to the Table

All who have confessed saving faith in Jesus Christ as their personal Lord and Savior are invited to receive the elements of bread and cup tonight. If you continue to believe in Christ, contine to repent of sin, and remain in fellowship with Christ's church, you may walk up to the table to receive the elements after which you may return to your seat and use the time for silent meditation and prayers.

✟ Receiving the Bread

The minister will indicate when it is time to receive the bread:

"On the night when he was betrayed, the Lord Jesus took a loaf of bread, and when he had given thanks, he broke it and said, 'This is my body, which is given for you. Do this in remembrance of me'" (1 Corinthians 11:23–24 NLT).

✝ Moments of Meditation

Solo: Silent Night or Beneath the Cross of Jesus (Option: print story of writing of hymn in program or project words on screen at front of sanctuary).

✝ Receiving the Cup

The minister will indicate when it is time to come to receive the cup:

"In the same way, he took the cup of wine after supper, saying, 'This cup is the new covenant between God and you, sealed by the shedding of my blood. Do this in remembrance of me as often as you drink it.' For every time you eat this bread and drink this cup, you are announcing the Lord's death until he comes again" (1 Corinthians 11:25–26 NLT).

✝ Moment of Meditation

As the instruments play the hymn Hark! the Herald Angels Sing or When I Survey the Wondrous Cross, reflect on the words printed below (or words can be projected on a screen at the front of the sanctuary).

✝ Recessional

Congregation stands as minister and elders/deacons recess.

✝ Postlude

Joy to the World or O Sacred Head Now Wounded

Contemporary Communion Ideas

Introduce the communion service with a brief message on the forgiveness which Christ provides through his death on the cross. Provide each person in the service with a piece of paper along with a pin or piece of tape. During a time of quiet reflection and prayer encourage the members of the congregation to write down any sin which they have found it difficult to believe that God has forgiven. Then invite those who come forward to receive the communion elements to walk to a cross near the communion table and attach their folded paper to the cross before proceeding to the table to receive the bread and cup. At the conclusion of the service remind people that they have been invited to leave their sin at the cross.

For an evening service during Holy Week, darken the sanctuary and place a wooden cross at the front of the room. As people enter the sanctuary, hand each of them a large squared nail to take to their seat and hold during the service. At the point in the service when the members of the congregation are invited to come to the table, ask participants to first walk to the cross and drop their nail into the basket at the foot of the cross before proceeding to the table to receive the elements. The sound of nails dropping into the basket serves as a powerful reminder that our sins nailed Christ to the cross.

Set up a table(s) at the front of the sanctuary with a dozen chairs around it. Invite people to come forward and fill the dozen chairs. The pastor or elder/deacon passes the bread to each person and offer a word of encouragement. Repeat the same process with the cup. An alternate suggestion is to use thirteen chairs, leaving one chair for the pastor to sit along with the group and pass the elements while seated. Once the first group has been served, they may return to their seats so the next group of twelve can come forward.

For an evening communion service in a sanctuary with movable seating, place tables throughout the room with chairs. If there is sufficient room it may work best to position the tables so that they form a "U" shape. Place candles on each table; subdued lighting contributes to an atmosphere of reverence. The communion elements can be passed from person to person seated at the tables. Some churches may prefer to begin the evening with a shared meal prior to beginning the worship time.

Provide variety by assigning participants to read Scripture passages the entire time in which the communion elements are being served. You may wish to use scripted readings from *The Dramatized Old Testament* or *The Dramatized New Testament* edited by Michael Perry (Baker Books). Or designate a music leader to lead the congregation in a cappella singing of the first stanzas of familiar hymns or songs in a pre-planned progression.

Use several unsliced loaves of freshly baked bread to pass from one person to the next. Ask each person to pull off a small piece from the loaf and then hold the loaf while the person sitting next to him/her is allowed to break off another piece.

During the passing of the communion elements, project slides of biblical art on a screen at the front of the sanctuary to accompany music. Scenic videos are also available which accompany contemporary praise songs or hymns. Video projectors can make it possible for these to be used even in large sanctuaries.

Some suggestions in this section have been contributed by James Emery White, Mecklenburg Community Church, Charlotte, North Carolina.

9

Believers' Baptism

Service One

✝ Scripture Reading

One or both of the following passages may be read:

"Jesus came and told his disciples, 'I have been given complete authority in heaven and on earth. Therefore, go and make disciples of all the nations, baptizing them in the name of the Father and the Son and the Holy Spirit. Teach these new disciples to obey all the commands I have given you. And be sure of this: I am with you always, even to the end of the age'" (Matthew 28:18–20 NLT).

"Well then, should we keep on sinning so that God can show us more and more kindness and forgiveness? Of course not! Since we have died to sin, how can we continue to live in it? Or have you forgotten that when we became Christians and were baptized

145

to become one with Christ Jesus, we died with him? For we died and were buried with Christ by baptism. And just as Christ was raised from the dead by the glorious power of the Father, now we also may live new lives. Since we have been united with him in his death, we will also be raised as he was. Our old sinful selves were crucified with Christ so that sin might lose its power in our lives. We are no longer slaves to sin. For when we died with Christ we were set free from the power of sin" (Romans 6:1–7 NLT).

Alternate text: Acts 8:26–28, 34–38

This may be followed by the pastor providing brief remarks about the ordinance of baptism and leading in prayer.

✝ Baptismal Questions

Each candidate for baptism is asked the following questions:

1. Do you confess that you know you are a child of God through exercising personal faith in the Lord Jesus Christ as your Savior from sin?
   I do.
2. Do you confess that your intention is to follow Christ in dying to selfish desires and living a life of obedience that pleases him?
   I do.
3. Do you desire to obey Christ's command to be baptized now?
   I do.

Optional: Each candidate is asked to give a personal word of testimony.

Baptism

N_____, upon your public confession of faith in the Lord Jesus Christ as Savior, and your professed desire to obey Christ by submitting to water baptism, I now baptize you in the name of the Father, the Son, and the Holy Spirit. Amen.

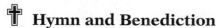 Hymn and Benediction

Service Two

✝ **Words of Introduction**

Listen to the words of Jesus Christ who said:

"If anyone would come after me, he must deny himself and take up his cross and follow me. For whoever wants to save his life will lose it, but whoever loses his life for me and for the gospel will save it" (Mark 8:34–35).

"If you confess with your mouth, 'Jesus is Lord,' and believe in your heart that God raised him from the dead, you will be saved. For it is with your heart that you believe and are justified, and it is with your mouth that you confess and are saved" (Romans 10:9–10).

Our Lord Jesus Christ instituted the ordinance (sacrament) of baptism when he said to his disciples: "All authority in heaven and on earth has been given to me. Therefore go and make disciples of all nations, baptizing them in the name of the Father and of the Son and of the Holy Spirit, and teaching them to obey everything I have commanded you. And surely I am with you always, to the very end of the age" (Matthew 28:18–20).

✝ Profession of Faith

Today we are grateful that the following persons have expressed their desire to obey the command of Christ to be baptized. Let me now ask each one to publicly profess their faith in Christ:

1. Do you believe in God the Father, Almighty, Maker of heaven and earth, and in Jesus Christ his only Son, our Lord, and in the Holy Spirit, the Lord and giver of life?
   I do.
2. Do you confess your need for forgiveness for your sin, and with a contrite heart, place your whole trust in the person and work of Christ for your salvation?
   I do.
3. Do you promise to make use of the spiritual resources which Christ has provided through his church to be a faithful follower of Christ from this day onward?
   I do.

Let us pray.

Our Father in heaven, we acknowledge that your Son established the ordinance of baptism. We ask that you will now look with favor on the one(s) who have now come to be baptized. May you ratify in heaven that which we now in obedience to your command do on earth. May the presence of your Spirit fill us at this special moment. Forgive us our sins as we pray in the name of our crucified and resurrected Christ. Amen.

✝ Administration of Baptism

N_____, by the authority of the Lord Jesus Christ, in whom you have confessed your faith, I baptize you in the name of the Father, and of the Son, and of the Holy Spirit. Amen.

May the blessings of the triune God be on you and dwell in your heart forever. To him who is able to keep you from falling and to present you before his glorious presence without fault and with great joy—to the only God our Savior, be glory, majesty, power, and authority, through Jesus Christ our Lord, before all ages, now and forevermore! Amen.

Service Three

✝ **Words of Explanation**

Inasmuch as our Lord and Savior Jesus Christ has given authority and commandment to his disciples to teach all nations, baptizing them in the name of the Father and of the Son and of the Holy Spirit; and has declared that he who believes and is baptized shall be saved, for with the heart man believes to righteousness and with the mouth confession is made to salvation. This person, having witnessed a credible profession before the officers, now comes forward to obey this commandment. And inasmuch as we baptize only with water, and administer the outward and visible sign, while the Lord himself alone baptizes with the Holy Spirit and with fire, and communicates the inward spiritual grace which washing with water signifies, let us now with one accord invoke the presence and blessing of God.

✝ **Prayer**

Most holy and merciful Father, when your Son our Lord and Savior gave commission to his disciples to teach all nations, baptizing them in your name, and teaching them all his commandments, he also promised to be with them always, even to the end of the world. In faith in this promise and in obedience to this commandment we present to you this your servant, who, repenting and renouncing all sin, accepts your salvation, and humbly desires to put on this sacramental seal and badge of discipleship. May the blood of Christ, who through the eternal Spirit offered himself without spot to God, purge his/her conscience from dead works to serve the living God. Baptize him/her, O Lord, we ask, with the Holy Spirit and with fire. Purify and purge him/her like gold and silver, that he/she may offer to the Lord an offering in righteousness.

As he/she is hereby enrolled with the soldiers of the cross, clothe him/her, we pray, with the whole armor of God—the breastplate of righteousness, the shield of faith, the helmet of salvation, and the sword of the Spirit—that his/her body protected with truth, and his/her feet covered with the preparation of the gospel of peace, he/she may be able to withstand in the evil day, and having done all to stand. And so mightily work in him/her by your light and power that he/she may be preserved from all error, and maintained in the patience, perseverance, and victory of your saints; so that his/her name may not be blotted out of your book of life, but that he/she may have place with those of every nation who, coming out of great tribulation, have washed their robes and made them white in the blood of the Lamb. Amen.

✝ Questions

Do you believe in God the Father Almighty, Maker of heaven and earth?

I do.

Do you believe in Jesus Christ his only Son, our Lord, who was conceived of the Holy Spirit, born of the Virgin Mary, suffered under Pontius Pilate, was crucified, dead and buried; who on the third day rose again from the dead; who ascended into heaven, and sitteth at the right hand of God the Father Almighty; from thence he shall come to judge the living and the dead?

I do.

Do you believe in the Holy Spirit, the holy catholic Church, the communion of saints, the forgiveness of sins, the resurrection of the body, and the life everlasting?

I do.

Is it your desire to be baptized in this faith?

It is.

Having confessed your sin, and having embraced Christ as your Savior, do you submit to him as your Teacher, and is it your purpose faithfully to obey and serve him as your Lord and Master as long as you live?

It is.

✝ Administration of Baptism

N_____, I baptize you in the name of the Father, and of the Son, and of the Holy Spirit. Amen.

Then the minister shall charge the newly baptized as follows:

Seeing, beloved, that you have now publicly professed your faith and received the sacramental seal of that covenant by which you are dedicated to Christ, and Christ with all the benefits of his redemption is made yours forever, give all diligence to make your calling and election sure; adding to your faith virtue, and to virtue knowledge, and to knowledge self-control, and to self-control patience, and to patience godliness, and to godliness brotherly kindness, and to brotherly kindness love; for if these things be in you and abound, they make you that you shall neither be barren nor unfruitful in the knowledge of our Lord Jesus Christ. For so an entrance shall be ministered to you abundantly into the everlasting kingdom of our Lord and Savior Jesus Christ.

And now, in the name of the Lord, I commend you as a member of the holy catholic Church to the confidence, the love, and the care of the brothers and sisters. And may the grace of our Lord Jesus Christ, and the love of God, and the communion of the Holy Spirit be with you forever. Amen.

Adapted from *Manual of Forms*, Archibald Alexander Hodge (Philadelphia: Presbyterian Board of Publication, 1882), pp. 22–25.

10

Infant Baptism and Dedication Services

Evangelical Service of Infant Baptism

✝ Words of Institution and Explanation

We're privileged today to baptize the child of one of our families. Baptism is a sacrament that's often been misunderstood. So let me explain briefly why we are baptizing the infant of believing parents in obedience to the command of Christ.

Our reason for baptizing infants is derived not from church tradition alone but also from the teaching of Scripture itself. The basis is found in God's initiative whereby he instituted a covenant with Abraham and his children. God's covenant promise contained spiritual blessings summarized in the guarantee: "I will be your God and you shall be my people" (Genesis 12:2–3; 17:1).

God commanded that the outward sign of this inner covenant be circumcision. This sign was to be administered to Abraham's descendants as God chose to work in family units. Genesis 17:7 reminds us that God's covenant with Abraham was intended to be "an everlasting covenant." So this covenant was still in effect generations later when Christ lived on earth. Galatians 3:14 states, "in order that in Christ Jesus the blessing of Abraham might come to the Gentiles, so that we might receive the promise of the Spirit through faith" (NASB). Those who exercise saving faith in Christ are now the true seed of Abraham. We have inherited God's covenant. Galatians 3:29 states, "If you belong to Christ, then you are Abraham's offspring, heirs according to promise" (NASB).

If we have now inherited this covenant, what should be the outward sign? Circumcision is no longer the commanded sign. Colossians 2:11–12 teaches that circumcision has been replaced by baptism as the sign of being in God's covenant.

Just as the sign was administered to believers and their children in the Old Testament, so the sign now may be administered to believers and their children. Peter said in Acts 2:39 (NASB), "the promise is for you and your children, and for all who are far off, as many as the Lord our God shall call to himself." Paul informs us in 1 Corinthians 7 that the children of at least one believing parent are holy. A child, chosen by God to be born into a home where parents believe in Christ, is exposed to special blessings. God's pattern has generally been to work in such families.

So to summarize, baptism is a sign that the child of believing parents is included in the blessings of the covenant of grace.

Baptism per se, however, does not regenerate a child. No magic in the water removes sin or guarantees admission into heaven. Just as outward circumcision alone was not effective without circumcision of the heart, so baptism alone is not effective. There is no ironclad guarantee of salvation to all who are baptized as children. Each baptized child needs to be exposed to the teachings of the Bible about salvation by grace and not by works. Each child needs to be encouraged to repent of sin and believe in Christ alone for salvation. When this does occur, we can rejoice at God's faithfulness to his covenant. What a privilege to administer this sign and seal of God's blessings, anticipating what he can continue to do in the life of this child.

✝ Confession of Faith

With these thoughts in mind, we'll now ask the parents to come forward.

Let me now ask you, N_____ and N_____, to affirm as parents your faith and intentions, both before the church family and in the presence of the Lord of this church. Please do so by answering "We do" after each question:

1. Do you acknowledge that you are saved from sin by grace through faith in Christ and not through anything you have done or ever will do?

2. Do you also acknowledge your child's need of the cleansing blood of Jesus Christ and the renewing grace of the Holy Spirit?
3. Do you come claiming God's covenant promises on behalf of your child, and do you look in faith to the Lord Jesus Christ for his/her salvation?
4. Do you now unreservedly dedicate your child to God, and promise, in humble reliance on his divine grace, that you will strive to set before him/her a godly example, that you will pray with and for him/her, that you will teach him/her the doctrines of the Christian faith, and that you will attempt to bring him/her up in the nurture and instruction of the Lord?

And now a question for you who are part of the church family. Training and raising a child is a bigger task than what parents can do alone. We need the help and encouragement of one another as we are willing to serve in the church. So let me raise this question: Do you the members of this church family undertake the responsibilities of assisting these parents in the Christian nurture of their child? If so, please answer, We do.

✝ Administration of Baptism

Let us pray: Father, we now administer the sign and seal of your promise. We do so acknowledging that you are our faithful God and we are your people. May your grace and blessings be upon this child and his/her parents. This we pray, believing in the work of Jesus Christ and in his holy name. Amen.

N_____, child of the covenant, I now baptize you in the name of the Father, and of the Son, and of the Holy Spirit. Amen.

✝ Baptismal Prayer

Presbyterian Service

✝ Opening Sentences

While the parents are bringing the children to be baptized a baptismal hymn may be sung; or the following sentences may be read by the minister.

The mercy of the Lord is from everlasting to everlasting upon them that fear Him, and His righteousness unto children's children;

To such as keep His covenant, and to those that remember His commandments to do them.

He shall feed His flock like a shepherd: He shall gather the lambs in His arms, and carry them in His bosom.

For the promise is unto you, and to your children, and to all that are afar off, even as many as the Lord our God shall call.

Glory be to the Father, and to the Son, and to the Holy Ghost; as it was in the beginning, is now, and ever shall be, world without end. Amen.

The minister shall say:

Dearly beloved, the Sacrament of Baptism is of divine ordinance. God our Father, who has redeemed us by the sacrifice of Christ, is also the God and Father of our children. They belong, with us who believe, to the membership of the Church through the covenant made in Christ, and confirmed to us by God in His Sacrament, which is a sign and seal of our cleansing, of our engrafting into Christ, and of our welcome in the household of God. Our Lord Jesus said, Suffer the little children to come unto Me, and forbid them not, for of such is the kingdom of God. Verily I say unto you, Whosoever shall not receive the kingdom of God as a little child, he shall not enter therein. And He took them up in His arms, and put His hands upon them and blessed them. Saint Paul also declared that the children of believers are to be numbered with the holy people of God.

Confession of Faith

The minister shall say:

In presenting your Child for baptism, do you confess your faith in Jesus Christ as your Lord and Savior; and do you promise, in dependence on the grace of God, to bring up your Child in the nurture and admonition of the Lord?

Then the answer is given:

I do.

Then the minister shall say:

Let us pray.

Most merciful and loving Father, we thank Thee for the Church of Thy dear Son, the ministry of Thy

Word, and the sacraments of grace. We praise Thee that Thou hast given us so gracious promises concerning our children, and that in mercy Thou callest them to Thee, marking them with this Sacrament as a singular token and pledge of Thy love. Set apart this water from a common to a sacred use, and grant that what we now do on earth may be confirmed in heaven. As in humble faith we present this Child to Thee, we beseech Thee to receive him, to endue him with Thy Holy Spirit, and to keep him ever as Thine own; through Jesus Christ our Lord. Amen.

✝ Administration of Baptism

All present reverently standing, the Minister shall say:

What is the Christian name of this Child?

Then the Minister, taking the Child in his arms, or leaving it in the arms of the Parent, pronouncing the Christian name of the Child, shall pour or sprinkle water upon the head of the Child saying:

N_____, I baptize thee in the name of the Father, and of the Son, and of the Holy Ghost. Amen.

The blessing of God Almighty, Father, Son, and Holy Ghost, descend upon thee, and dwell in thine heart for ever. Amen.

✝ Congregational Response

Then the Minister shall say to the congregation:

This Child is now received into Christ's Church: And you the people of this congregation in receiving this Child promise with God's help to be his sponsor to the end that he may confess Christ as his Lord and Saviour and come at last to His eternal kingdom. Jesus said, Whoso shall receive one such little child in My name receiveth Me.

✝ Prayers

Then the Minister shall say:

Let us pray.

Almighty and everlasting God, who of Thine infinite mercy and goodness hast promised that Thou wilt be not only our God, but also the God and Father of our children: We humbly beseech Thee for this Child, that Thy Spirit may be upon him, and dwell in him for ever. Take him, we entreat Thee, under Thy Fatherly care and protection; guide him and sanctify him both in body and in soul. Grant him to grow in wisdom as in stature, and in favor with God and man. Abundantly enrich him with Thy heavenly grace: bring him safely through the perils of childhood, deliver him from the temptations of youth, and lead him to witness a good confession, and to persevere therein to the end.

O God our Father, give unto Thy servants whom Thou hast committed this blessed trust, the assurance of Thine unfailing providence and care. Guide them with Thy counsel as they teach and train their child; and help them to lead their household into an ever-increasing knowledge of Christ, and a more steadfast obedience to His will.

We commend to Thy Fatherly care the children and families of this congregation. Help us in our homes to honor Thee, and by love to serve one another.

And to thy name be all blessing and glory, through Jesus Christ our Lord. Amen.

And now, as our Savior Christ hath taught us, we humbly pray . . . *(The Lord's Prayer)*

Then the Minister shall say:

The grace of the Lord Jesus Christ, and the love of God, and the communion of the Holy Spirit, be with you all. Amen.

Methodist Service

✝ **Words of Introduction**

The minister coming to the font, which is to be filled with pure water, shall say:

Dear friends in Christ:

God, through Moses, made covenant with Israel, saying to the people, "And these words which I command you this day shall be upon your heart; and you shall teach them diligently to your children, and shall talk of them when you sit in your house, and when you walk by the way, and when you lie down, and when you rise."

In the days of the New Covenant, Christ Jesus said, "Let the children come to me and do not hinder them; for to such belongs the kingdom of heaven"; and on the day of Pentecost the Apostle Peter declared, regarding the salvation given through Christ, "The promise is to you and to your children."

It is therefore our privilege to present our children to the Lord and our duty to raise them in His ways. These parents now bring this child to offer him/her in dedication and to pledge in the presence of this congregation, to bring him/her up in the Lord's discipline and instruction.

✝ Prayer

Let us pray: Almighty and everlasting God, who has made saving covenant with Your people and who, out of Your lovingkindness, has ordained that they should live before You in families; we thank You that it is our privilege to dedicate our children to You, in steadfast hope that they will cleave to Your covenant and live to Your glory. We entreat You for this child that he/she may be delivered from the power of sin and Satan and be set apart to You by the power of the Holy Spirit. We pray for these parents that they may be given divine aid, so that both by instruction and example they may lead this child in the way of everlasting life, and so all may come in unity together to Your eternal kingdom. We pray for this congregation, that we may faithfully discharge our duties to both parents and child, through Jesus Christ our Lord. Amen.

✝ Baptismal Promises

Questions to parents:

1. Do you, in the presence of God and this church, solemnly dedicate this child to the Lord?
   Answer: We/I do.
2. Do you, so far as you are able on his/her behalf, renounce the devil and his works, the lure of the world and the sinful desires of fallen man, so that in the training of this child you will not be led by them and so that, as far as

you are able, you will keep this child from following them?
Answer: We/I do.

3. Will you faithfully strive by word and example to lead this child to personal faith in Christ?
Answer: We/I will.

4. Do you accept the authority of the Old and New Testaments?
Answer: We/I do.

5. Out of them, will you diligently teach this child the commandments and promises of the Most High God, raising him/her in the discipline and instruction of the Lord?
Answer: We/I will.

The congregation will now stand. Let us acknowledge our duty to strengthen this family with prayers and encouragement, thus aiding both parents and child to fulfill all that has here been promised.

✝ Administration of Baptism

The pastor shall here take the child, and say:

N_____, I baptize you in the name of the Father, and of the Son, and of the Holy Spirit. Amen.

✝ Prayers

Let us pray: O God, from whom every family on heaven and on earth is named, grant that this child may increase in wisdom and stature, growing in favor with You and with man. So guide and uphold these parents that they may lead this child into that life of faith in Jesus Christ whose mark in this world is righteousness and in the world to come, everlasting bliss. May he/she be brought early to affirm in faith all that has here been pledged on his/her behalf, through Jesus Christ our Lord. Amen.

Benediction: "Now to Him who is able to keep you from falling and to present you without blemish before the presence of His glory with rejoicing, to the only God, our Savior through Jesus Christ our Lord, be glory, majesty, dominion, and authority, before all time and now and for ever. Amen" (Jude 24–25).

In the place of the second prayer, the minister may offer an extemporaneous prayer which will include the petitions set forth in the printed prayer.

From *Pastor's Handbook* (Indianapolis: The Board of Bishops of the Free Methodist Church [USA], 1994), pp. 105–7. Scripture quotations from the RSV.

Service of Infant Dedication

✝ Words of Explanation

Dear friends in Christ:

God, through Moses, made covenant with Israel, saying to the people, "And these words which I command you this day shall be upon your heart; and you shall teach them diligently to your children, and shall talk of them when you sit in your house, and when you walk by the way, and when you lie down, and when you rise."

In the days of the New Covenant, Christ Jesus said, "Let the children come to me and do not hinder them; for to such belongs the kingdom of heaven"; and on the day of Pentecost the Apostle Peter declared, regarding the salvation given through Christ, "The promise is to you and to your children."

It is therefore our privilege to present our children to the Lord and our duty to raise them in His ways. These parents now bring this child to offer him/her in dedication and to pledge in the presence of this congregation, to bring him/her up in the Lord's discipline and instruction.

✝ Prayer

Let us pray: Almighty and everlasting God, who has made saving covenant with Your people and who, out of Your lovingkindness, has ordained that they should live before You in families—we thank You that it is our privilege to dedicate our children to You, in steadfast hope that they will cleave to Your covenant and live to Your glory. We entreat You for this child that he/she may be delivered from the power of sin and Satan and be set apart to You by the power of the Holy Spirit. We pray for these parents that they may be given divine aid, so that both by instruction and example they may lead this child in the way of everlasting life, and so all may come in unity together to Your eternal kingdom. We pray for this congregation, that we may faithfully discharge our duties to both parents and child, through Jesus Christ our Lord. Amen.

✝ Questions to Parents and Congregation

1. Do you, in the presence of God and this church, solemnly dedicate this child to the Lord?
   Answer: We/I do.
2. Will you endeavor to live a life before this child which will give witness to your faith in Jesus Christ?
   Answer: We/I will.
3. Do you accept the authority of the Old and New Testaments as the Word of God?
   Answer: We/I do.

4. Out of them, will you endeavour diligently to teach this child the commandments and promises of the Most High God, so that your child may early come to personal faith in Jesus Christ? *Answer: We/I will.*

Let us acknowledge our duty to support this family with our prayers and encouragement, thereby aiding both parents and child to fulfill all that has been promised. The congregation will affirm this by standing.

✝ Dedication and Prayer

The minister shall take the child in his arms and shall say:

Even as Joseph and Mary brought Jesus in the time of His infancy to the temple to present Him to God, so now, in the name of the Lord Jesus Christ, we present N_____ in an act of dedication to God, with a prayer that at an early age in life he/she may experience His justifying and sanctifying grace. Amen.

Here the minister shall pray an extemporaneous prayer on behalf of the parents and their child.

From *Pastor's Handbook* (Indianapolis: The Board of Bishops of the Free Methodist Church [USA], 1994), pp. 109–10. Scripture quotations from the RSV.

Baby Blessing and Parent Dedication

✝ Explanation

N_____, you have brought this child, N_____, into this sacred place of worship for God's anointment and your dedication of yourselves to rear the child in the Christian way of life.

It has scriptural precedent, for Jesus our Lord, as a baby, was brought by Mary and Joseph to the Temple, where the prophet Simeon took Him in his arms, blessed Him according to their custom, and they dedicated themselves to the sacred responsibility.

This is a service of thanksgiving to God for the joy and hope that has come into their lives by the presence of this child. It is recognition of God as the Giver of Life and an affirmation that all children are His. It is a reconsecration of yourselves.

The love of a home will help determine his/her future characteristics. God will enrich his/her life, if you will keep the doors of your own lives open to God.

✝ Questions

Do you dedicate your child to God? Answer: *We do*.

Do you promise to give your child the best that you have learned of the ways and love of your Heavenly

Father, so that he/she may grow into the love and nurture and admonition of the Lord? Answer: *We do.*

Pastoral Prayer

Heavenly Father, gracious and merciful, we thank you that you have given these the privilege of parenthood, and have blessed their home with this little life.

Bless this child, O Lord, with strength of body, soundness of mind, and health of soul.

Help these parents to keep Christian values, to develop Christian priorities, and to walk in the paths committed to faith, truth, justice, and righteousness so that this child may grow toward you. Grant them patience and wisdom, good judgment and balance for this demanding task, in the name of Jesus Christ. *(Pastor takes baby in arms.)*

This is N_____ born _____. The paternal grandparents are N_____. The maternal grandparents are N_____.

Blessing Prayer

"The LORD bless you and keep you: the LORD make his face to shine upon you, and be gracious to you: the LORD lift up his countenance upon you, and give you peace [throughout your life. Amen]" (Numbers 6:24–26 RSV).

Adapted from James L. Christensen, *The Complete Handbook for Ministers* (Grand Rapids: Fleming H. Revell, 1985), pp. 183–84.

11

Confirmation and Public Profession of Faith

Evangelical Confirmation Service

✝ **Address to the Congregation**

Brothers and sisters in Christ: just as nature has its times and seasons, each of which is important, so in the providence of God does human nature. There is a time to be born and a time to die; a time to plant and a time to harvest; a time for the early and the latter rain. This is most certainly true. Thanks be to God!

Today we rejoice because our youth are on the same gracious pilgrimage in the faith as we are—having been drawn by God's Word, by holy example, by the sacraments, and by prayer. We know that their journey has only begun. Yet we are confident that he who began a good work in them will bring it to completion in the day of Jesus Christ.

Let us give thanks to him who awakens faith in them and in us.

 Profession of Faith

Here the minister may invite the confirmands to rise as their names are called and, when they are all standing, to come forward.

The Apostles' Creed has generally been accepted by the Christian church in all ages as a worthy affirmation of its faith. I invite you now to share with the congregation in that affirmation by responding to the following questions:

All or part of the following should be included in the bulletin for the day to allow for full participation.

Minister: Do you believe in God.

All: I believe in God, the Father almighty, creator of heaven and earth.

Minister: What does this mean?

All: It means that God has created me and all that exists. He has given me, and still preserves, my body and soul with all their powers. He provides me with food and clothing, home and family, daily work, and all I need from day to day. God also protects me in time of danger and guards me from every evil. All this he does out of fatherly and divine goodness and mercy, though I do not deserve it. Therefore I surely ought to thank and praise, serve and obey him. This is most certainly true!

Minister: Do you believe in Jesus Christ?

All: I believe in Jesus Christ, his only Son, our Lord. He was conceived by the power of the Holy Spirit, and born of the Virgin Mary. He suffered under Pontius Pilate, was crucified, died, and was buried. He descended to the dead. On the third day he rose again. He ascended into heaven, and is seated at the right hand of the Father. He will come again to judge the living and the dead.

Minister: What does this mean?

All: It means that Jesus Christ—truly God, Son of the Father from eternity, and truly man, born of the Virgin Mary—is my Lord. He has redeemed me, a lost and condemned person, saved me at great cost from sin, death, and the power of the devil—not with silver or gold, but with his holy and precious suffering and death. All this he has done that I may be his own, live under him in his Kingdom, and serve him in everlasting righteousness, innocence, and blessedness, just as he is risen from the dead and lives and rules eternally. This is most certainly true!

Minister: Do you believe in the Holy Spirit?

All: I believe in the Holy Spirit, the holy catholic Church, the communion of saints, the forgiveness of sin, the resurrection of the body, and the life everlasting.

Minister: What does this mean?

All: It means that I cannot by my own understanding or effort believe in Jesus Christ, my Lord, or come to him. But the Holy Spirit has called me through the Gospel, enlightened me with his gifts, and sanctified and kept me in true faith. In the same way he calls, gathers, enlightens, and sanctifies the whole Christian Church on earth, and keeps it united with Jesus Christ in the one true faith. In this Christian Church, day after day, he fully forgives my sins and the sins of all believers. On the last day he will raise me and all the dead and give me and all believers in Christ eternal life. This is most certainly true!

Following this recitation, the minister may address the confirmands as follows:

Confession of Personal Faith

This the church of Christ believes. As your pastor and teacher, it is my prayer that it may also be your personal confession and the basis for the commitment of your life to Jesus Christ as your Savior and Lord.

Answering only for yourself, and in perfect freedom to be silent if you cannot yet answer "I do," I now call upon you to respond to the following questions:

Do you believe with the Church of Jesus Christ that the Bible, the Old and New Testaments, is the Word of God—telling the story of God and his people in the past and guiding them today? If so, answer "I do."

I do.

As a member of this confirmation class, do you affirm your place as a giving and receiving friend in this congregation of Christians?

I do.

As you continue in your life, do you intend to keep worshipping, in Christ's church, listening to his Word, and responding to Christ's call, according to your faith?

I do.

Do you confess personal faith in Jesus Christ and desire, with God's help, to be his disciple?

I do.

So be it, according to your faith.

As the class kneels for prayer it is appropriate for significant adults in their lives—other teachers and/or parents, sponsors, the diaconate, church members chosen by the confirmands—to gather around them, placing hands on their heads as the pastor prays for them one by one.

Free, personal prayer, prepared in advance with each confirmand in mind, is appropriate. Otherwise a common prayer may be repeated for each, with slight variations from person to person depending on the number involved.

Let us pray.

Heavenly Father, we thank you today for N_____, and the gift of his/her life among us. Grant us in this moment to be sensitive to this person and his/her potential for good in your world. Grant him/her, in turn, the grace of true faith in you, real love for your people, and abiding trust in your promises; through Jesus Christ our Lord. Amen.

An alternative to the prayer for each individual would be one prayer for the entire group—again, either free prayer, carefully thought through beforehand with the group in mind, or as follows:

Let us pray.

Lord God, our maker, redeemer, and friend, we thank you today for the confessions of faith which these, your children, have made—according to their own personal experience of you. How grateful we are that you know them all and that you love and understand each one.

We commend them to you now, having given them your Word, praying that you will seal it on their hearts and in their minds. Lead them to do justly and to love mercy and to walk humbly with their God. Keep them from sin, and help them to grow willingly in the grace and knowledge of our Lord Jesus Christ.

Surround them, we pray, with signs of your triumph, especially when they are tempted to fall away. And give them grace, while they are young and strong, to become the servants you want them to be.

Through Jesus Christ our Lord, who taught us when praying to say:

Here the class and congregation shall unite in the Lord's Prayer.

The minister shall say:

The Lord bless you and keep you; the Lord make his face to shine upon you, and be gracious to you; the Lord lift up his countenance upon you, and give you peace. Amen.

*The confirmands will stand. A personal word of congrat-
ulations by the minister or a selected lay leader is appropriate, after which, as their names are announced, a cer-
tificate of confirmation may be presented to each class
member.*

Hymn

Savior, While My Heart Is Tender

✟ Benediction

Now to the One who can keep you from falling and
set you in the presence of his glory, jubilant and above
reproach, to the only God our Savior, be glory and
majesty, might and authority; through Jesus Christ
our Lord, before all time, now, and for evermore.
Amen.

From *The Covenant Book of Worship,* vol. 3 (Chicago: Covenant
Press, 1978), pp. 232–39.

Christian Reformed Public Profession of Faith

✞ Words of Introduction

Congregation of our Lord Jesus Christ:

Today we are privileged to welcome into the full life of the church's fellowship those who wish to confess their faith in Christ as Lord and Savior. When they were baptized God made clear his claim on them as his own, and they were received into the church. Now they wish to share fully in the life of this congregation and of the whole church of God. And so today they will publicly accept and confirm what was sealed in their baptism, confess their faith in the Lord Jesus, and offer themselves to God as his willing servants. We thank God for having given them this desire and pray that as we now hear their confession, he will favor us with the presence and guidance of his Holy Spirit.

✞ The Vows

N_____, will you stand now, and in the presence of God and his people respond to the following questions:

1. Do you believe that Jesus Christ is the Son of God sent to redeem the world, do you love and trust

him as the one who saves you from your sin, and do you with repentance and joy embrace him as Lord of your life?

Answer: I do.

2. Do you believe that the Bible is the Word of God revealing Christ and his redemption, and that the confessions of this church faithfully reflect this revelation?

Answer: I do.

3. Do you accept the gracious promises of God sealed to you in your baptism and do you affirm your union with Christ and his church which your baptism signifies?

Answer: I do.

4. Do you promise to do all you can, with the help of the Holy Spirit, to strengthen your love and commitment to Christ by sharing faithfully in the life of the church, honoring and submitting to its authority; and do you join with the people of God in doing the work of the Lord everywhere?

Answer: I do.

✝ The Reception

The minister asks the congregation to rise.

Minister: In the name of our Lord Jesus Christ I now welcome you to all the privileges of full communion. I welcome you to full participation in the life of the church. I welcome you to its responsibilities, its joys, and its sufferings. "May the God of peace, who through the blood of the eternal covenant brought back from the dead our Lord Jesus, that great Shepherd of the sheep, equip you with everything good for doing his will, and may he work in us what is pleasing to him, through Jesus Christ, to whom be glory for ever and ever. Amen" (Hebrews 13:20–21).

Congregation: Thanks be to God! We promise you our love, encouragement, and prayers.

Minister: Let us together say what we believe:

[Here follows the Apostles' Creed in unison.]

✝ The Prayer

Lord, our God, we thank you for your Word and Spirit through which we know Jesus Christ as Lord and Savior. May those who confessed your name today never cease to wonder at what you have done for them. Help them to continue firmly in the faith, to bear witness to your love, and to let the Holy Spirit shape their lives. Take them, good Shepherd, into your care that they may loyally endure opposition in serving you. May we, with all your children, live together in the joy and power of your Holy Spirit. We ask this, Lord Jesus, in the hope of your coming. Amen.

From *Psalter Hymnal* (Grand Rapids: CRC Publications, 1987), pp. 964–65.

12

Anointing the Sick

Service One

Scripture tells when we are ill to call the Elders of the church and let them pray over us. Elders are instructed to anoint the sick person with oil in the name of the Lord. Having spent time in prayer, the Elders are to go to the sick person to pray for his/her healing with the anointing of oil.

✝ Prayer

Our Lord Jesus Christ gave the invitation, "Come to me, all of you who are weary and carry heavy burdens, and I will give you rest. Take my yoke upon you. Let me teach you, because I am humble and gentle, and you will find rest for your souls. For my yoke fits perfectly, and the burden I give you is light" (Matthew 11:28–30 NLT).

With this in mind, let us pray.
Dear God and Father of our Lord Jesus Christ, Father of compassion and God of all comfort, we con-

fess that you are our refuge and strength, an ever present help in trouble. Therefore we will not fear. Help us to be still and know that you are God. You will not grow tired and weary. You give strength to the weary and increase the power of the weak. Those who hope in you will renew their strength. They will soar on wings like eagles, they will run and not grow weary, they will walk and not faint. We come this day to pray for N_____. May your grace be sufficient for him/her and your power be made perfect in his/her weakness. Increase our faith in your power to heal. Increase our desire to submit to your sovereign will. This we pray in the name of Jesus Christ and in the power of your Holy Spirit who is now among us. Amen.

The Lord's Prayer (Optional)

✝ Scripture Reading

"Praise the Lord, O my soul; all my inmost being, praise his holy name. Praise the Lord, O my soul, and forget not all his benefits—who forgives all your sins and heals all your diseases; who redeems your life from the pit and crowns you with love and compassion, who satisfies your desires with good things so that your youth is renewed like the eagle's" (Psalm 103:1–5).

"All praise to the God and Father of our Lord Jesus Christ. He is the source of every mercy and the God who comforts us. He comforts us in all our troubles so that we can comfort others. When others are troubled, we will be able to give them the same comfort God has given us. You can be sure that the more we suffer for

Christ, the more God will shower us with his comfort through Christ. So when we are weighed down with troubles, it is for your benefit and salvation! For when God comforts us, it is so that we, in turn, can be an encouragement to you. Then you can patiently endure the same things we suffer. We are confident that as you share in suffering, you will also share God's comfort.

We are pressed on every side by troubles, but we are not crushed and broken. We are perplexed, but we don't give up and quit. We are hunted down, but God never abandons us. We get knocked down, but we get up again and keep going. Through suffering, these bodies of ours constantly share in the death of Jesus so that the life of Jesus may also be seen in our bodies. . . . we never give up. Though our bodies are dying, our spirits are being renewed every day. For our present troubles are quite small and won't last very long. Yet they produce for us an immeasurably great glory that will last forever! So we don't look at the troubles we can see right now; rather, we look forward to what we have not yet seen. For the troubles we see will soon be over, but the joys to come will last forever" (2 Corinthians 1:3–7; 4:8–10, 16–18 NLT).

Option: Sing Hymn

✝ Confession of Sin and Words of Assurance

The New Testament exhorts us, "confess your sins to one another, and pray for one another, so that you may be healed. The effective prayer of a righteous man can accomplish much" (James 5:16 NASB). Let us now pause as we silently confess our sins before the Lord. *(If oral confession is appropriate, public sins may be confessed publicly, and personal or private sins may be confessed privately.)*

Hear God's gracious promise of forgiveness: "The LORD is compassionate and gracious, slow to anger, abounding in love. He will not always accuse, nor will he harbor his anger forever; he does not treat us as our sins deserve or repay us according to our iniquities. For as high as the heavens are above the earth, so great is his love for those who fear him; as far as the east is from the west, so far has he removed our transgressions from us. As a father has compassion on his children, so the LORD has compassion on those who fear him" (Psalm 103:8–13).

✝ Anointing with Oil

The elders of the church gather around the believer who has requested this anointing. Clear olive oil in a small container may be used to anoint on the forehead.

We have gathered at your request and in keeping with the instructions of the New Testament as recorded in James 5:13–16:

"Is any one of you in trouble? He should pray. Is anyone happy? Let him sing songs of praise. Is any one of you sick? He should call the elders of the church to pray over him and anoint him with oil in the name of the Lord. And the prayer offered in faith will make the sick person well; the Lord will raise him up. If he has sinned, he will be forgiven. Therefore confess your sins to each other and pray for each other so that you may be healed. The prayer of a righteous man is powerful and effective."

A brief exposition of the passage might be appropriate at this point.

Let us pray.

Our gracious God, the source of all healing, in Jesus Christ you possess the power to heal all sickness and to restore to health. We thank you for this oil given to us as a sign of healing and forgiveness. By the power of your Spirit come upon the one who will be anointed with oil that he/she might receive your touch and be made whole, to the glory of Jesus Christ our Redeemer. We submit to your sovereign will as we pray in the name of your Son. Amen.

N_____, we anoint you in the name of the Father, and of the Son, and of the Holy Spirit.

As you are outwardly anointed with oil, may our heavenly Father grant you the inward anointing of his Spirit. May he in mercy grant you forgiveness of your sins, release from your sufferings, and restoration to health and strength. May he deliver you from all evil, grant you the ability to accept his sovereign will, and bring you to everlasting life, through Jesus Christ our Savior and Lord. Amen.

✝ Prayers of Petition and Thanksgiving

Several elders and others, including the individual who has been anointed, may pray for God's healing and give

*thanks for his perfect will which is sufficient in all cir-
cumstances, however God may choose to respond to our
prayers. They may choose to lay hands on the sick person
while praying.*

Sing Doxology (or Hymn):
Praise God from whom all blessings flow,
praise him all creatures here below,
praise him above ye heavenly hosts,
praise Father, Son, and Holy Ghost. Amen.

✝ Benediction

"And now, may the God of peace, who brought
again from the dead our Lord Jesus, equip you with
all you need for doing his will. May he produce in
you, through the power of Jesus Christ, all that is
pleasing to him. Jesus is the great Shepherd of the
sheep by an everlasting covenant, signed with his
blood. To him be glory forever and ever. Amen"
(Hebrews 13:20–21 NLT).

Service Two

The healing of the body, mind, and spirit is an act of the God who is both Creator and Redeemer. It can be sought only in the Spirit of Christ, who prayed, "Not my will but yours be done." The service of healing should be used only after the congregation has been fully prepared.

As part of The Service for the Lord's Day the act of healing can come at the time of the petitions and intercessions, or it can be a special service focusing on healing. It may also take place in a home or a hospital with representatives of the congregation present, along with the minister.

✝ Scripture Reading

The service begins as the minister reads from the following or other suitable Scripture passages: 2 Kings 4:8–37; Psalm 23; 91; 103; 145:13b–18; Matthew 4:23; 8:1–4; 8:5–13; 8:14–17; 9:2–8; Mark 6:7–13; 10:46–52; Luke 17:11–19; John 9:1–12; Acts 3:1–10; 16:16–18; Hebrews 12:1–2; James 5:13–16; 1 John 5:13–15.

The minister may then interpret the passages read and present some words concerning health and healing. If the service is included in a worship service, the minister invites any who desire healing to come forward and kneel

190

or stand beside the minister, indicating the need for which prayer is desired.

✝ Prayer

The minister then prays extempore for that person's special need, or as follows:

We praise you, Merciful God, for the loving care that you have given to N_____. We now come before you with his/her special need. If it be in accord with your will, may he/she be restored to fullness of health. This mercy we pray in the name of Jesus Christ who brought healing and wholeness to those who came to him with outstretched arms and open hearts. Amen.

✝ Anointing

If it is the custom of the congregation, the minister may anoint with oil the person requesting healing. After the anointing the minister shall lay his or her hands upon the sick person's head and say:

Let us pray.

Eternal God, who sent Jesus Christ into the world to bring health and liberty to all, by that same power wherein he healed the sick, minister now to N_____. Grant that he/she may be delivered from sickness and be brought to health. Give him/ her grace to receive whatever is given to him/her, knowing that with you all things work together for good to those who love you. Amen.

✝ Benediction

After a time of silence the minister says:

May the God of peace be with you. And may your spirit, mind, and body be made whole in the presence of Jesus Christ. Amen.

From *A Manual of Worship: New Edition,* John E. Skoglund and Nancy E. Hall (Valley Forge: Judson Press, 1993), pp. 256–58. Reprinted with permission.

13

Recognition of Births
and Adoptions

✝ Hymn

Lord of Life and King of Glory
Jesus, Friend So Kind and Gentle

✝ Call to Thanksgiving
for the Birth of a Child

Dear Friends: The birth of a child is a joyous and
solemn occasion in the life of a family. It is also an
occasion for rejoicing in the Christian community. I
bid you, therefore, to join N_____ and N_____ in giving thanks to Almighty God our heavenly Father, the
Lord of all life, for the gift of N_____ to be their
son/daughter (*BCP*, 1979).

✝ Call to Thanksgiving
for the Adoption of a Child

Dear Friends: It has pleased God our heavenly
Father to answer the earnest prayers of N_____ and
N_____, member(s) of this Christian family, for the
gift of a child. I bid you join with them in offering

heartfelt thanks for the joyful and solemn responsibility which is theirs by the coming of N_____ to be a member of their family. But first, our friends wish us, here assembled, to witness the inauguration of this new relationship (*BCP*, 1979).

To the parents:

N_____ and N_____, do you take this child for your own?

We do.

If the child is old enough to answer:

N_____, do you take this woman as your mother?
I do.
Do you take this man as your father?
I do.

Then, holding or taking the child by the hand, give the child to the mother or father saying,

As God has made us his children by adoption and grace, may you receive N_____ as your own son (daughter).

One or both parents say these or similar words:

May God the Father of all, bless our child N_____, and us who have given to him our family name, that we may live together in love and affection; through Jesus Christ our Lord. Amen.

✝ Scripture Reading

- Matthew 18:1–5 (NLT) "The disciples came to Jesus and asked, 'Which of us is greatest in the

Kingdom of Heaven?' Jesus called a small child over to him and put the child among them. Then he said, 'I assure you, unless you turn from your sins and become as little children, you will never get into the Kingdom of Heaven. Therefore, anyone who becomes as humble as this little child is the greatest in the Kingdom of Heaven. And anyone who welcomes a little child like this on my behalf is welcoming me.'"

- Deuteronomy 6:4–9
- 1 Samuel 1:9–11, 19b–20
- Psalm 8
- Mark 10:13–16
- Luke 1:47–55
- Luke 2:22–40

✝ Prayer

Gracious Lord, who has entrusted this child to the care of this family, we thank you for our salvation through Jesus Christ our Lord. Give grace that he/she may grow up to have a healthy body, a believing heart, and an obedient mind, loving your Word and following its direction.

We pray that they may together attend the services of your church, follow the instructions of your Word, and teach the child to know the Scriptures and to love you and your Son, Jesus Christ.

Help this mother and father (brother and sister) to perform their duties as a family to set a worthy example by their lives. Help all of us to remember that we are temples of your Holy Spirit and that the greatest expression of Christ in our lives is love shared with one another.

We pray these things in the name of Jesus Christ, your Son, the friend of children, and Savior of us all (From *The Covenant Book of Worship, vol. 3,* pp. 278–79).

O God, you have taught us through your blessed Son that whoever receives a little child in the name of Christ receives Christ himself: We give you thanks for the blessing you have bestowed upon this family in giving them a child. Confirm their joy by a lively sense of your presence with them, and give them calm strength and patient wisdom as they seek to bring this child to love all that is true and noble, just and pure, lovable and gracious, excellent and admirable, following the example of our Lord and Savior, Jesus Christ. Amen (*BCP,* 1979).

Almighty God, giver of life and love, bless N_____ and N_____. Grant them wisdom and devotion in the ordering of their common life, that each may be to the other a strength in need, a counselor in perplexity, a comfort in sorrow, and a companion in joy. And so knit their wills together in your will and their spirits in your Spirit, that they may live together in love and peace all the days of their life; through Jesus Christ our Lord. Amen (*BCP,* 1979).

The Lord's Prayer

✝ Hymn

Children of the Heavenly Father
Doxology

✝ Benediction

"And now, may the God of peace, who brought again from the dead our Lord Jesus, equip you with all you need for doing his will. May he produce in you, through the power of Jesus Christ, all that is pleasing to him. Jesus is the great Shepherd of the sheep by an everlasting covenant, signed with his blood. To him be glory forever and ever. Amen" (Hebrews 13:20–21 NLT).

14

Groundbreaking and Church Dedications

Groundbreaking Service

✝ Invocation

Lord God, Almighty, we come before you in the name of Jesus Christ who is the builder and cornerstone of the church. You have called us to be part of your visible church on earth which you are continuing to build. As we gather to break ground for the construction of a facility in which we can meet, we pray that you will unite us in Christ to accomplish your purposes. Direct all of the planning and construction which shall take place on this site. Continue to work in our hearts so that when the building is completed we may use it fully in ways that will advance your work in the hearts of people. This we pray in the name of Christ and with the help of the Holy Spirit who indwells us. Amen.

✝ Hymn

The Church's One Foundation
Christ Is Made the Sure Foundation

✝ Words of Welcome and Purpose

Set aside time for remarks by the pastor, building committee chairman, or board chairman, which may include the story of how the Lord has led the congregation to this special landmark occasion. This may also include an introduction of special guests present for the occasion.

✝ Scripture Reading

Select one of the following:
    1 Chronicles 29:10–16
    Ezra 3:10–13
    Psalm 24:1–6
    Psalm 95:1–7
    1 Corinthians 3:9–14
    1 Peter 2:4–12

✝ Prayer of Thanksgiving

Leader: We have gathered as a church recognizing the grace of God which has brought us to this special point in our life together.

People: We now break ground to the glory of our God.

Leader: And in grateful remembrance of his past and present blessings on our church family.

People: We come with confidence in his ability to continue to do immeasurably more than all we ask
or imagine.

Leader: According to his power that is now at work
within our church.

People: We now break ground in order that we might
build a structure in which we can assemble for
worship, instruction, and fellowship, and then
go forth to serve in our community and the world
in which we have been called to live.

Leader: With God's help we will build, asking,

People: May the favor of the Lord rest upon us;

Leader: Establish the work of our hands for us.

People: Yes, establish the work of our hands so Christ
might be glorified in this church throughout all
generations. Amen.

✝ Act of Groundbreaking

The first person to turn over a shovel of earth may say:

In the name of the Father, the Son, and the Holy
Spirit, we break this ground. Amen.

*Then the shovel is handed to the others which may
include appropriate officers and representatives of var-
ious age groupings in the church, community or denominational representatives, architect, and building
contractor.*

Option following groundbreaking:

Minister: Now, with the Lord's help and by his grace,
let us build. And all God's people say:

People: Amen.

✝ Doxology

✝ Prayer

The pastor and/or other selected individuals may lead in prayer and may conclude with the Lord's Prayer.

✝ Hymn

Great Is Thy Faithfulness
To God Be the Glory
O for a Thousand Tongues to Sing
Lead On, O King Eternal
I Love Thy Kingdom, Lord
Forth in Thy Name, O Lord, I Go

✝ Benediction

"And now, may the God of peace, who brought again from the dead our Lord Jesus, equip you with all you need for doing his will. May he produce in you, through the power of Jesus Christ, all that is pleasing to him. Jesus is the great Shepherd of the sheep by an everlasting covenant, signed with his blood. To him be glory forever and ever. Amen" (Hebrews 13:20–21 NLT).

Service of Building Dedication

✟ **Musical Prelude**

✟ **Welcome and Recognition of Guests**

✟ **Hymn**

Christ Is Made the Sure Foundation
The Church's One Foundation
Not unto Us, O Lord

✟ **Prayer of Invocation**

Lord God, who has called us into fellowship with your Son Jesus Christ, please look with favor on us this special day in the life of N_____ church. Our hearts are overflowing with thanksgiving as we reflect back on all that has transpired to bring us to this day in the life of this church family. We know that even the heavens can't contain you, let alone a human structure such as this. Yet you delight to live in the hearts of people who are devoted to you and are part of your church. We come to recognize the ways in which your hand has been at work in our lives. Cleanse our hearts, we pray, from all sinful thoughts and desires. May you come among us on this day to receive our expressions of gratitude. May Jesus Christ be honored in this new building and in this service of dedication. This we pray in the name of our Lord. Amen.

✝ Solo or Choral Selection

✝ Scripture Reading

One or more of the following selections may be read:

1 Kings 8:22–30
1 Chronicles 29:10–19
Psalm 48
Psalm 84
Matthew 7:13–14, 24–25
Matthew 21:10–14
Ephesians 2:14–22
Ephesians 4:11–16
1 Corinthians 3:1–11, 16–17
1 Peter 2:1–10

✝ Dedicatory Sermon

✝ Hymn

O Thou Whose Hand Has Brought Us
May Jesus Christ Be Praised
How Great Thou Art
We Dedicate This Temple

✝ Presentation of Keys

By architect, contractor, or chairman

✝ Act of Dedication

Leader: We have assembled this day to set apart this building to be a house of God. We believe that God has put it into our hearts to erect this church. We know that he has guided our minds and strengthened our hands for the task.

People: So we in N____church have assembled with gratitude and joy to consecrate this building,

Leader: To the everlasting God, our Father, in whom we live and move and have our being, from whom comes every good and perfect gift, who so loved the world that he gave his only begotten Son.

People: We dedicate this building,

Leader: To Jesus Christ, our Lord and Savior, who loved us and gave himself for us in his death on the cross, who rose and lives forevermore as the way, the truth, and the life.

People: We in N____church dedicate this building,

Leader: To the Holy Spirit, our comforter and guide, by whom alone is wrought the renewal of the heart.

People: We dedicate this building,

Leader: For worship in prayer and praise; for the ministry of the Word and the proclamation of the gospel of Jesus Christ; for the administration of the holy ordinances (sacraments); for the missionary endeavor of the church; for community outreach to touch the lives of many people till the return of our Lord Jesus Christ.

People: We dedicate this building,

Leader: For the instruction of children, youth, and adults in the truths of the Christian faith; for the strengthening of the family; for comfort to those who mourn and strength to those who are tempted, we set apart this building.

Unison: We the people of N___church now consecrate ourselves anew to the worship of God and the service of others. We dedicate this building and all its furnishings with thanksgiving in the name of the Father, and of the Son, and of the Holy Spirit. Amen.

✝ **Solo or Choral Selection**

✝ **Dedicatory Prayer**

✝ **Gloria Patri**

✝ **Dedicatory Offering**

✝ **Hymn**

Glory to God! Praise to Thy Holy Name!
To God Be the Glory
Great Is Thy Faithfulness
Lead On, O King Eternal

✝ **Benediction**

Appendix A

Church Year Calendars and Personal Worship Cycles

✝ The Cycle of the Church Year

- **Advent** (four Sundays)
  Season of expectation
  ROYAL BLUE OR PURPLE
- **Christmas Season**
  Season of fulfillment
  WHITE OR GOLD
    Christmas Eve
    Christmas Day
    First and second Sundays after
      Christmas Day
- **Epiphany Season** (January 6)
  Season of revelation
  GREEN
    Up to eight Sundays
- **Lent** (forty weekdays and six Sundays)
  Season of penitence
  PURPLE
    Ash Wednesday
    Six Sundays
    Holy Week

Season of passion
 BLACK
  Palm/Passion Sunday
  Maundy Thursday
  Good Friday
  Holy Saturday (Easter vigil)
- **Easter** (fifty days with seven Sundays)
 Season of celebration
  WHITE OR GOLD
   Seven Sundays
   Ascension Day
   Pentecost Sunday
  RED
- **Season after Pentecost** (Ordinary Time)
 Season of growth
  GREEN
   Trinity Sunday
   Up to twenty-five Sundays

Table for Finding Special Days

Year	Lent	Easter	Pentecost	Advent
1999	Feb. 17	Apr. 4	May 23	Nov. 28
2000	Mar. 8	Apr. 23	June 11	Dec. 3
2001	Feb. 27	Apr. 14	June 2	Dec. 1
2002	Feb. 13	Mar. 31	May 19	Dec. 1
2003	Mar. 5	Apr. 20	June 8	Nov. 30
2004	Feb. 24	Apr. 11	May 30	Nov. 28
2005	Feb. 9	Mar. 27	May 13	Nov. 27
2006	Mar. 1	Apr. 16	June 4	Dec. 1
2007	Feb. 21	Apr. 8	May 27	Dec. 2
2008	Feb. 5	Mar. 23	May 11	Nov. 30
2009	Feb. 25	Apr. 12	May 31	Nov. 29
2010	Feb. 17	Apr. 4	May 23	Nov. 28
2011	Mar. 9	Apr. 24	June 12	Nov. 27
2012	Feb. 21	Apr. 8	May 27	Dec. 2
2013	Feb. 13	Mar. 31	May 19	Dec. 1
2014	Mar. 5	Apr. 20	June 8	Nov. 30
2015	Feb. 18	Apr. 5	May 24	Nov. 29
2016	Feb. 9	Mar. 27	May 15	Nov. 27
2017	Mar. 1	Apr. 16	June 4	Dec. 3
2018	Feb. 14	Apr. 1	May 20	Dec. 2
2019	Mar. 6	Apr. 21	June 9	Dec. 1
2020	Feb. 25	Apr. 12	May 31	Nov. 29
2021	Feb. 17	Apr. 4	May 23	Nov. 28
2022	Mar. 2	Apr. 17	June 5	Nov. 27
2023	Feb. 22	Apr. 9	May 28	Dec. 3
2024	Feb. 13	Mar. 31	May 19	Dec. 1
2025	Mar. 5	Apr. 20	June 8	Nov. 30

Monthly Cycle of Acts and Attributes for Personal Worship

Day	Theme	Day	Theme
1	God's act of creation	17	The Triune God is just
2	God's act of election	18	The Triune God is light
3	Christ's incarnation	19	The Triune God is living
4	Christ's acts of shepherding	20	The Triune God is loving
5	Christ's redemption	21	The Triune God is merciful
6	Christ's resurrection	22	The Triune God is omnipotent
7	Christ's ascension	23	The Triune God is omnipresent
8	Holy Spirit's coming at Pentecost	24	The Triune God is omniscient
9	Christ's return	25	The Triune God is patient
10	The Triune God is beautiful	26	The Triune God is sovereign
11	The Triune God is eternal	27	The Triune God is truthful
12	The Triune God is faithful	28	The Triune God is unchanging
13	The Triune God is good	29	The Triune God is unified
14	The Triune God is great (majestic)	30	The Triune God is wise
15	The Triune God is holy		
16	The Triune God is jealous		

Seven-Week Cycle of Daily Psalter Readings from the *Book of Common Prayer*
(49-Day Journey through the Book of Psalms)

	Day	A.M.	P.M.		Day	A.M.	P.M.		Day	A.M.	P.M.
WEEK ONE	Sun	146, 147	111, 112, 113	**WEEK TWO**	Sun	148, 149, 150	114, 115	**WEEK THREE**	Sun	63, 98	103
	Mon	1, 2, 3	4, 7		Mon	25	9, 15		Mon	41, 52	44
	Tue	5, 6	10, 11		Tue	26, 28	36, 39		Tue	45	47, 48
	Wed	119:1–24	12, 13, 14		Wed	38	119:25–48		Wed	119:49–72	49, 53
	Thu	18:1–20	18:2; 1–50		Thu	37:1–18	37:19–42		Thu	50	59, 60
	Fri	16, 17	22		Fri	31	35		Fri	40, 54	51
	Sat	20, 21	110, 116, 117		Sat	30, 32	42, 43		Sat	55	138, 139
WEEK FOUR	Sun	24, 29	8, 84	**WEEK FIVE**	Sun	93, 96	34	**WEEK SIX**	Sun	66, 67	19, 46
	Mon	56, 57, 58	64, 65		Mon	80	77, 79		Mon	89:1–18	89:19–52
	Tue	61, 62	68		Tue	78:1–39	78:40–72		Tue	97, 99, 100	94, 95
	Wed	72	119:73–96		Wed	119:97–120	81, 82		Wed	101, 109	119:121–141
	Thu	70, 71	74		Thu	83	85, 86		Thu	105:1–22	105:23–45
	Fri	69	73		Fri	88	91, 92		Fri	102	107:1–32
	Sat	75, 76	23, 27		Sat	87, 90	136		Sat	107:33–43	108, 33
WEEK SEVEN	Sun	118	145								
	Mon	106:1–18	106:19–48								
	Tue	120, 121, 122	123, 124, 125								
	Wed	119:145–176	128, 129, 130								
	Thu	131, 132, 133	134, 135								
	Fri	140, 142	141, 143								
	Sat	137, 144	104								

Appendix B

Worship Planning Forms

Weekly Worship Planning Sheet

Date of Service:

☑ Worship theme

☑ Sermon thesis

☑ Sermon Scripture text

☑ Other Scripture readings and method

☑ Sermon response ideas

☑ Call to worship ideas

☑ Music selections

☑ Musicians

☑ Hymns/songs

☑ Creeds/confessions

☑ Drama or visual elements (banners, art objects, etc.)

☑ Instructions for sanctuary setup

☑ Visual ideas for bulletin cover

☑ Participants

Name	Responsibility

Annual Worship Planning Overview

Year: _____

Sunday	Scripture	Sermon	Worship Theme
January			
1			
2			
3			
4			
5			
February			
1			
2			
3			
4			
March			
1			
2			
3			
4			
5			
April			
1			
2			
3			
4			
5			
May			
1			
2			
3			
4			
5			

Appendix B

Sunday	Scripture	Sermon	Worship Theme
June			
1			
2			
3			
4			
5			
July			
1			
2			
3			
4			
5			
August			
1			
2			
3			
4			
5			
September			
1			
2			
3			
4			
5			
October			
1			
2			
3			
4			
5			

Sunday	Scripture	Sermon	Worship Theme
November			
1			
2			
3			
4			
5			
December			
1			
2			
3			
4			
5			

Appendix C

Worship Service Evaluation Chart

Date and time of service _____

Key: 1 Significant lack   4 Above average
        2 Needs attention   5 Excellent
        3 Good but could improve

1	2	3	4	5	
					Does your worship service have a logical, smooth flow from one part to the next?
					Does the order and content of the service reflect the theological stance of your church/denomination?
					Is adequate provision made for visitors to understand and participate in what is occurring?
					Do the worship leaders communicate both reverence and enthusiasm?
					How would you evaluate the singability of the music used in the service?
					Is there a noticeable connection between the sermon and the rest of the service?
					Is the sermon an appropriate length?
					Is there a noticeable connection between choral/special music and the rest of the service?

1	2	3	4	5	
					Does the order of service ever change?
					How would you evaluate the effectiveness of the sound system?
					How would you evaluate the effectiveness of the printed information handed out in the service?

Please answer the following questions:

- What percentage of music in the service consists of traditional hymns? _____

  _____

  _____

- What percentage of music in the service consists of contemporary praise/Scripture songs?_____

  _____

  _____

- What methods of Scripture reading are used in services?

  _____

  _____

  _____

- What are some ways Scripture is used in the service in addition to the Scripture reading time? _____

  _____

  _____

217

List the parts of your worship service in the vertical column on the left side. Then after each item fill in the columns with a yes or no or with a check mark. Calculate the percentage in the bottom row.

Parts of service	Standing	Sitting	Leader participating	Congregation participating	Horizontal— toward people	Vertical— toward God
Percentages						

Worship Service Evaluation Chart

What is most effective about your church's worship services?

_____

_____

_____

What is least effective?_____

_____

_____

_____

Appendix D

Contemporary Worship Music and Drama Resources

Sources for Contemporary Worship Music

Antara Music
P.O. Box 1240
Anderson, IN 46012
(800) 468-7232

Brentwood Music
468 McNally Drive
Nashville, TN 37211-3318
(800) 333-9000
http://www.goshen.net/
  Brentwood

Fred Bock Music
P.O. Box 1240
Anderson, IN 46012

Celebration
P.O. Box 309
Aliquippa, PA 15001
(800) 722-4879

Chordant Music
400 Capitol Way
P.O. Box 1029
Jacksonville, IL 62650
(800) 877-4443

Christian Music Online
P.O. Box 14904
Fremont, CA 94539
(510) 490-0282
http://www.cmo.com

Gaither Music Co. (Praise
  Gathering)
P.O. Box 737
State Road 9 South
Alexandria, IN 46001
(800) 666-1330

Genevox Music Group
MNS114
127 Ninth Avenue North
Nashville, TN 37234
(800) 844-7712

G.I.A. Publications
7404 S. Mason Avenue
Chicago, IL 60638
(800) 442-1358

Good News Music Service
10415 Beanslee Blvd.
Bothell, WA 98011
(800) 821-9207
http://www.gnms.com

Hope Publishing Company
380 South Main Place
Carol Stream, IL 60188
(800) 323-1049

Hosanna Integrity Music
101 Winners Circle
Brentwood, TN 37024
(800) 877-4443

Integrity
P.O. Box 11483
Birmingham, AL 35202
(800) 240-9000

Lillenas Publishing Company
Box 419527
Kansas City, MO 64141
(800) 877-0700

Maranatha Music
P.O. Box 31050
Laguna Hills, CA 92654-1050
(800) 444-4012

Mercy Music
Box 65004
Anaheim, CA 92815

Tempo Music
P.O. Box 1240
Anderson, IN 46012
(800) 468-7232

Wellsprings Unlimited
204 Stevens Court
Burnsville, MN 55337
(612) 890-3863

Word Music
3319 W. End Ave. Suite 200
Nashville, TN 37203
(615) 385-9673
http://www.wordrecords.com

Worship Works
National Worship Resource
 Network
10619 Alameda Drive
Knoxville, TN 39932
(615) 966-0103

Drama for Worship

Baker Book House
Box 6287
Grand Rapids, MI 49516-6287
(800) 877-2665
http://www.bakerbooks.com

Communication Resources, Inc.
4150 Belden Village Street,
 4th Floor
Canton, OH 44718
(800) 992-2144
http://www.comresources.com

Good News Music Service
http://www.gnms.com/drama.htm

Lamb's Players Theatre
P.O. Box 26
National City, CA 91951

Lillenas Publishing
2923 Troost Avenue
Kansas City, MO 64109
(800) 877-0700

Reformed Worship
CRC Publications
2850 Kalamazoo SE
Grand Rapids, MI 49560
(800) 333-8300

Word Publishing
1501 LBJ Freeway, Suite 650
Dallas, TX 75234-6069
(800) 251-4000

Zondervan—Willow Creek
  Resources
5300 Patterson Avenue SE
Grand Rapids, MI 49530
(800) 876-7335
http://www.zondervan.com

Music Copyright Licensing

Christian Copyright Licensing
International (CCLI)
17201 NE Sacramento Street
Portland, OR 97230
(800) 234-2446 (SongSelect
  Software)
http://www.ccli.com

LicenSing
Copyright Cleared Music for
Churches
(800) 328-0200

Request for Permission to Copy

Name of publisher _____

Address _____

_____

Name of church _____

Contact person _____

Address _____

_____

Phone _____ FAX _____

We request permission to copy the following for which you own the copyright:

1. Title and number _____

2. Name of book in which it is found _____

_____

3. We plan to use

_____ Text only

_____ Music only

_____ Both text and music

4. We would like to use it for the following

_____ Church bulletin for use on _____(date) for

the following number of copies _____

_____ Overhead transparency/slide for repeated use

_____ Other

- -

Publisher's approval by _____

Date _____ Fee _____

_____

Paul E. Engle is an ordained minister who has served in pastoral ministry in churches in Pennsylvania, Connecticut, Illinois, and Michigan. Dr. Engle has also taught as a visiting instructor in the practical theology departments of Trinity Evangelical Divinity School, Knox Theological Seminary, and Reformed Theological Seminary. He earned degrees from Houghton College, Wheaton Graduate School, and Westminster Theological Seminary. His doctoral work focused on the area of worship. He conducts seminars in churches on the subject of corporate worship.